Story Matters

Empowering Your Hope
While Going Through Tough Times

Transformational Stories
Compiled by Linda A. Olson

Amazon #1 Bestseller

Copyright © 2021 by Linda A. Olson.

All rights reserved. This book is protected by copyright. No part of this book may be reproduced or transmitted in any form or by any means, including as photocopies or scanned-in or other electronic copies, or utilized by any information storage and retrieval system without written permission from the copyright owner.

Interior Design by FormattedBooks.com

ISBN: 978-0-9819014-5-9

Published by Made for More Publishing,
an arm of Made for More Enterprises, Inc.

Printed in the United States of America.

Acknowledgments

In this volume of
***Story Matters: Empowering Your Hope
While Going Through Tough Times,***
many thanks are extended to:

—**my grandchildren,** who were the inspirations to write.
Christine Schat
from The Tree of Faith

—**my fiancée, Andy Wojciechowski**, for staying right next to me every day through this tough journey. For you, I can keep fighting with a smile.
Hatsuki Murata
from Facing the Storm with Kokoro

—**my sons, Raymond and Samuel**, who loved me and supported me as a mother through every high and low. Because of you, I am growing and learning to become a better person.
Leena Ying Tang
from Soar Like An Eagle

—**my son, Jason,** who has been my inspiration and support, for your loving guidance as I've grown older.

Joanne Peters
"Moving Mom and Dad"

—**my daughter, Sydney**, who taught me more about embracing adversity in her short life than I may have learned in a lifetime. I am blessed to carry on her legacy.

Victoria Chapin
"Sydney's Dash"

—**my friend, Taning Conner**, for her commitment and unfailing faith in me."

Teresa Campbell
"Uniquely Yours"

—**my parents, Abe & Lena Bergen**, who never gave up, even when the struggle was almost unbearable. They are now celebrating with Billy in heaven.

Linda Olson
from *Transform Your Story*

—**Jesus Christ** for Your abundant grace. You are the One who made the seemingly impossible, possible. You are the One who sacrificed Your life on the cross so we could enjoy life and life more abundantly. From the depths of our hearts, we say, "Thank You"!

Dear Reader...

Do you ever wonder if you are making a difference in the world today? Have you ever looked at your labors and wondered if *anything* you were doing mattered to anyone else? Are you making the kind of impact you would like to make in the lives of others? Does your life—your *story*—matter?

Of course, it does. Each of the amazing women who share their stories in this volume was in the same place in life, wondering if society was any better because of their efforts. Each woman took a long look at her life and decided to change her story. And by changing her story, each woman changed her world.

These very personal accounts share several themes:

- ❖ *Each woman* faced the great emotional storms of adversity and discovered ways to rise above them.
- ❖ *Each woman* embraced her story, refusing to blame others for her troubles, and took full responsibility to persevere through tough times.

❖ *Each woman* refused to stay "stuck in her story" and, with heels dug in and eyes looking unwaveringly forward, followed her dream.

Was it easy? No, not at all. These courageous women, facing major challenges, learned through strength, courage, and personal faith in Jesus Christ that they could rise above nearly-impossible circumstances to discover great fulfillment.

As you read through these pages, consider your own life, your own story. What would it take to change the way you spend your days? How would it feel to know that *your* story impacted the lives of others so that they too decided to change?

Everyone has a story, and *your* story can bring transformation and impact into the world today. Dig into your life's message and discover the power of story to change lives, including your own.

Remember—*your story matters!*

Linda

* * * *

Transform *your* story into a life-changing message to the world!

Here are a few resources I have created for you:

- Register for a FREE 5-Day Storytelling Challenge with Linda. Go to http://wealththroughstories.com/story-challenge.
- Watch the *Wealth Through Stories* series on the FTG Network (ROKU) to meet some of the women you read about in this book. See channelstorie.roku.com.
- Experience story first-hand. Join Linda—and other storytellers—at *Wealth Through Stories LIVE*, a two-day story retreat. To learn more about WTS LIVE, go to http://wealththroughstories.com/story-retreat. Add the coupon code found in the back of this book for $100 off.

Are you **CONTINUALLY** plagued with **GUILT**?

Does **SHAME** drive you into deep emotional **DARKNESS**?

Have you **LOST ALL HOPE** of living freely, unhindered, and with great peace and joy?

PICK UP YOUR COPY AT AMAZON.COM

C.J. Schat, Amazon Best-selling author, shares the treasures she uncovered, after many painful years, in her book,
**The Tree of Faith:
God Wants to Answer Your Prayer**

In this book you will discover the:

- age-old secret to obliterating fear, guilt, and shame.
- personal way God answers questions.
- transforming power that heals deep wounds.
- unique key to turning life around.
- growing faith that looks past the impossible.

Contents

Acknowledgments iii

Dear Reader. v

Chapter 1 God Wants To Answer Your Prayer 1

Chapter 2 Will You Give Up Everything For Me? 17

Chapter 3 How Can I Face Another Storm? 29

Chapter 4 The Power of Forgiveness 45

Chapter 5 Uniquely Yours 57

Chapter 6 Sydney's Dash 73

Chapter 7 His Ways Are Higher 93

Chapter 1

God Wants To Answer Your Prayer

By Christine Schat

"God, help!"

Have you ever prayed this, the simplest of prayers? Have you ever been so desperate, so lonely, so despairing that you didn't know if you could even take another step, let alone know which direction to walk?

I've been there. Many times.

Every single one of us feels empty, incomplete at one time or another. We search diligently, work tirelessly, and sometimes walk directly into danger, all in the hopes of finding out how life really works.

Life works because of the Life-Giver.

Let me introduce you to Him.

After my sister Patti's death, I began to seriously seek God. I didn't know how to do that except to get involved in volunteer work at church. I would take little Joe to the church preschool, and I would do the necessary tasks involved in running the Sunday School program and midweek youth meetings. It took quite a bit of organizational effort. And, of course, I started going to church every Sunday.

Once a year was "Pledge Sunday" when small cards were distributed to the congregation and each of us was asked to make a financial pledge for the year's work of the church. No biblical teaching about giving was provided but, even so, I learned through that decision-making process that God's a giver.

You know what that means, don't you? If you are a follower of Christ—if you have repented and told God so and received His gift of eternal life—then, according to Romans 8:28-29, you are on your way to being conformed to the image of Christ. And Christ gave. So, you'd better become a giver in like manner: joyous, generous, and disciplined. You can give all you want, just don't give less than what He wants brought into His house: the tithe, the ten percent.

How did I learn the importance of the minimal tithe to Him? It's a pretty cute story, really. Before I became a "real" Christian, I was a nominal Christian—"form without power" as the scriptures say. It wasn't deliberate; I just didn't know any better. I believed, but I was longing for more. So, I became a little more involved in the church as part of my quest.

As I said, on Pledge Sunday, the ushers passed out cards to each person or family to record a commitment of a certain number of dollars to the church for the coming year. "Hmm," I said to my husband Joe Sr., who was even less "nominal" than I was, in the hopes that he would allow me to pledge something, even a little something.

You must understand that at the time we were living just a tad above the official poverty line. To help meet the expenses of raising three children, we had landed a part-time job doing janitorial chores at an apartment complex in the area. The job worked out well for us because I could continue to be a stay-at-home mom and do some of the work for the part-time job, and Joe could fill in after his regular work hours on the "fix-it" chores since we both knew that being mechanical is not one of my talents. We were careful with our finances but always just squeezing by—certainly we had no extras. The extra dollars the job provided were a godsend, as they say. And, as it turned out, a godsend in ways I couldn't foresee.

My husband's response to my request to pledge something was to name an astonishing dollar amount—one-third of this new part-time income! It took me two days to work through my emotions on that one. *We really need that money!* My heart cried at first. But I finally concluded that to refuse to give it was due to either selfishness on my part or fear of not having our needs met and continuing to be broke. I didn't feel that I could offer either excuse to God as a point of refusal, since the excuses boiled down to self-centeredness and lack of trust in Him, so I agreed, albeit reluctantly.

A week or so after that, my husband came home and told me that he had changed his mind, that the amount of the pledge that he had first mentioned was simply too much. As I tell you this next thing, you will see that God was definitely involved in this entire transaction. At the moment of my husband's statement, I was reading Ecclesiastes 5:4-5 which says, "When thou vowest a vow unto God, defer not to pay it; for he hath no pleasure in fools: pay that which thou hast vowed. Better is it that thou shouldest not vow, than that thous shouldest vow and not pay" (KJV). God had my attention! I shared what I was reading with Joe, and now God had Joe's attention too. We began the giving!

A couple of years later, after I had become a "real" Christian, passionately in love with God and wanting to please Him in every way, I was doodling around with our income numbers at tax time and realized, to my astonishment, that the amount of that original pledge was an exact ten percent of what our gross income had been at that time. God knew. We didn't. Ten percent is the biblical amount God calls his people to give into his work. In Malachi 3:8 he scolds his people for not giving. He called it "robbing God".

We have an interesting addendum to this story too. Several years later, after faithfully tithing, Joe decided he wanted to quit tithing altogether. Was he discouraged? Greedy? Rebellious? I didn't know, but we quit tithing. What Joe didn't know was that the kids and I were praying that God would show Joe the error of his decision.

A week later I was driving early on a Sunday morning on a Los Angeles freeway. Traffic was light, which was good because I began to feel dizzy, and so I started to move the car toward the emergency lane so that I could safely park. Never made it.

I passed out, unconscious, with the car still moving. Driverless, the car drifted across four lanes and crashed into the center concrete divider. I woke up lying on the car floor, motor still running.

No injuries.

The kicker was that the cost of repairing the car was the same as a year's tithe. Joe figured it out without any help from me.

There's an old saying in Christian circles: "If you don't give God what's his, the devil will steal it."

Yup!

* * * *

At some point during my college years, I remember making an appeal to God—*if* He was really there.

This was my request: "If You really exist and are really there for us humans, I want to know!"

Looking back, I see that the motive of my prayer was to know if I was alone in the universe. Alone in the big sense. I knew I had family, so I wasn't talking about that kind of alone.

"Are you there, God? Do you care? If so, please show me."

That was in the mid '60s, and I was in my mid-twenties. My next request came in the mid-'70s. And the answer took a year to arrive. He had to do some prep work in me first. Smile.

My sister, Patti, was gone and, since I had had the dream about her life after death, I wanted to know more about a possible afterlife—more about the "God-thing". I started going back to church and I read the Bible from cover to cover. Yep, the whole thing. I had the newly translated, paraphrased version called The Living Bible. For the first time, I started at the beginning of the book and didn't get defeated by the "begats"—you know, the genealogies that seem to go on forever. The paraphrased language and sentence structure was "American" and, for me, very helpful. Old King James's English vocabulary was a few centuries old and difficult to understand.

Anyway, I read it—a bit every morning. When I finished it, I made that next request: "God, if this is true, I want to know You, and I want every decision I make to be based on Your will, not mine, as I'm not doing very well on my own."

That was it. No lightning or thunder or anything like that. Life went on as usual—husband and kids and cleaning and cooking and so on.

And then things began to happen. The first thing was that we began to tithe our income, as I mentioned before. I began to do a lot of volunteer work at the church for the first time in my life, and people started giving me books to read that, if they were true, were absolutely amazing. The books told stories of people being healed, of people falling in love with God, of lives and attitudes being transformed. And these stories were not centuries old; they were current events. I was not buying all of it, but I was intrigued.

So I kept reading the books. And the Bible. And considering. And making decisions. I remember one day thinking that I would like to die. It wasn't that anything was so bad. It's just that I didn't think life had anything better to offer me than what I had already experienced, so why continue? I made the choice to stay because of family, of course. But for myself, there was just emptiness inside.

About this time, I also investigated other religions and found some intellectual appeal but no real "life" appeal. I wanted a God with whom I could have relationship—and the other religions didn't offer that.

Then toward the end of that year, a man in our congregation began telling stories to anyone who would listen about God doing miracles in his life. He was a former Marine, a tough guy from World War II, and he claimed his back had been miraculously healed and that he knew others who were having miraculous answers to prayers as well. He sounded just like the books I'd been reading. I listened to him from a distance as he told his stories to others. Part of me thought he was just too weird and yet, at the same time, I felt drawn to listen.

Also during that year, I experienced memories of situations where I had failed other people or hurt them in some way. It wasn't big stuff, but it was there. I had an inner quietness about it all, and I found myself agreeing that I needed some changing. God calls that whole process "salvation". He knew I was a sinner and He invited me to come to Him. I was saved from myself, and aware of a change that only He could accomplish in me.

I didn't understand all that at the time—I had no vocabulary for the change that was happening inside me—but God didn't need my understanding to do the working.

Anyway, all these things just kept being stirred in my "spiritual soup pot" over the course of about a year. I finally made the declaration to God that I wanted every decision in my life from that time forward to be according to His will, not mine. My ways weren't working very well.

* * * *

In the days that followed, I felt transported to a new level of life. As I walked around my neighborhood, I noticed that the sun shone brighter, the leaves sparkled, and people were beautiful.

It was as if a veil had been removed from over my being and life was bright. The seed of faith planted so many years ago, which He had so faithfully fed and watered, had finally burst through the soil and was greeting the *son*light. I had such joy! I'd never before experienced it in my life. Happiness, yes. But that would always depend on my circumstances. This was different. And such inner energy! I'd always been healthy and full of physical vitality, but this energy came from inside the core of my being.

I had many questions about this new-to-me faith, and now I posed my questions to Him directly. Answers, along with understanding, came to my mind. Then, just so I knew without a doubt that I wasn't making it up, I came across written material within a day or two that gave me the exact same answer I'd already come to understand. Confirmation.

And so I grew to trust this inner, quiet conversation with God's spirit. Amazing. But even more amazing to me was that I *knew* he loved me. Me? Yes, me. I found myself saying that out loud several times a day in a voice filled with the wonder of it.

He *loves* me! *He* loves me! He loves *me!*

And I wanted to tell everybody about the wonder of this God-person and His love.

Eventually, I began to teach in the church, starting with toddlers in preschool and working up to senior groups. I was surprised about the senior citizens wanting to listen to what I myself was learning because I was only in my mid-thirties. I think that they kept me on for a long time because of my passion for God and His word. It was contagious. I taught for several years and, as every teacher knows, it's the teacher who learns the most.

I loved it. And I loved Him because He first loved me (1 John 4:19). And, dear reader, He wants the opportunity to show you how He loves you! Go for it. Just ask! He'll take you on the journey to Himself.

* * * *

Psalm 40 speaks of being lifted out of a horrible pit. I believe that, for me, the horrible pit was life without knowing God, without having His life in me. A death life. Then, in verse 2, the psalmist describes what was in the pit: "miry clay". Just imagine yourself attempting to walk, run (not), sit down, or sleep in thick, deep, wet soil—soil so thick that, if it were to dry, it would be as hard as a brick. *That* is miry clay, and the psalmist describes the rescue as being lifted from the miry clay. The captive is out of the pit but still struggling simply to walk, making slow progress. Undoing bad habits. Building godly character. Learning to trust God. Learning to trust fellow believers. Forsaking anger, self-pity, condemnation, and so on. Finding no place to rest comfortably. But the ex-captive doesn't want to go back to the pit, so he keeps pressing onward.

I've had a few "miry clay" experiences in my life—times when I learned to trust God with everyday events.

My third child, Joe Jr., his cousin Sheri, and the neighbor's child were three tiny toddlers less than a year apart in age. My job was to take care of all three. The other mothers worked in the marketplace, and I worked at home.

Here's the kicker: I lived on the second floor of an apartment building. The only outdoor play area was a central courtyard that contained an unfenced pool—not safe for toddlers. So we spent almost all our time in the front area of my apartment, which amounted to about four hundred square feet. Sheesh!

For the most part, we had a good time. I let them play, kept them from bashing one another, fed them, and didn't bother to straighten up anything until their mothers had collected them. But one day I could feel that I was cranky—slugging through my own path of miry clay. Not in a mood for dirty diapers and dripping noses and squabbles over toys.

So I prayed, "Lord, if you see that I'm about to react too strongly to these little guys, please stop me." Now, that seems like a reasonable request, does it not? I wasn't worried about abusing them; I just didn't want to verbally snap at them or grab one in impatience.

The morning proceeded normally, peacefully. Then one of the little tykes picked up a toy and was about to bash one of his playmates. I said, "No, don't do that!" in a strong voice. That didn't stop her. My temper flared. Argh! I started to go over to grab her—in anger—to stop her from bashing her playmate.

And God remembered my prayer. As I took a step, my feet tangled in one another. Now this is strange because I am quite a physically capable person. Honest! I can walk. I'm a jogger. I played some sports. I'm not overweight or a weakling. But my feet tangled! And I went down flat on my face on the floor, breath knocked out of me. The kids were so surprised that they stopped squabbling to stare at me. And then we all laughed. Praise God, I had enough humility to say, "Thank you, Lord, for answering my prayer."

And here is another little-kid story: sometimes worse is on the way to better.

I had asked the Lord to take away our little Joey's desire to suck a pacifier. He was pushing three years old and still loved that thing. I was learning that emotional attachments needed to be handled gently, so I didn't want to just take it away and forbid him to have it anymore.

So I prayed about it, asking the Lord for a solution. Scripture says, "Don't worry about anything, but pray about everything" (Philippians 4:6), so I did. Why not?

Well, it got worse. He had that thing in his mouth every waking minute. "Lord, this is not what I had in mind," I complained. "I want him to like it *less,* not more!" But he sucked, and then he sucked some more, day after day.

And then it broke.

"Mommy, can I have another one?" he asked sadly, showing me the severed parts.

"Sweetie, I don't have any more."

"Oh."

He never asked again. Never complained. Didn't seem to mind.

And I began to learn that truly, God's ways are not my ways (Isaiah 55:9).

I lived in Los Angeles when I first became a Christian in the mid-seventies. Traffic was and is unbelievable, as you can imagine. Streets and freeways are never empty. People are in a hurry, caught up in their own anxieties, schedules, rushing, stressing, and so on. You get the picture. So, like many, I had done my fair share of cursing.

Well, once God's spirit was in me, I was no longer comfortable shouting at other drivers who frightened or frustrated me. So, what now? How should I handle it? Say nothing?

The answer that sprang into my mind was to use the occasion as an opportunity to pray for them. So I began to discipline myself to do that. No big deal. Just pray a simple prayer for God to meet their needs, keep them safe, introduce Himself to them. In short, bless them as He saw fit.

I found it surprisingly easy to do, and then I was even more surprised to see how many more people did unusual things in their cars around me. One of the most common was that someone would pull in front of me, and then slow way down. Noticeably. Irritatingly. And then I would remember that I wanted to change my response, and so I would pray. Many times, as soon as I prayed, the driver would pick up speed and go on his way. Soon, the irritations and my prayerful response became kind of a game for me. Fun.

Another part of my prayer life was not fun, however. I'd been praying for seven years over a situation that just kept getting worse. Harmful. Painful to others. Really bad. Worse than I knew at the time. I was discussing it with God one day as I was driving down the 405 freeway.

"You know, Lord, "I've been praying earnestly for a long time and nothing gets better. So let me ask You, 'Why should I think that these little, itty-bitty, one-time prayers that I pray over other drivers make any difference at all?' I'm just wasting my breath as far as I can tell." As soon as my thought was completed, the driver in the lane to my right sped up a bit and pulled in front of me. The driver behind him pulled ahead and was positioned a bit in front of me to the right. And the same thing happened in the left lane. The car that had been alongside me was now in a forward position and still on the left. The three cars in their individual lanes were all in a row directly in front of me. Each of those cars had a bumper sticker with a Christian slogan on it. All three. All at the same time. All escorting me down the freeway.

I laughed. "Okay, God. I guess it does make a difference!"

By the way, God also taught me how to obtain victory in the seven-year prayer as well.

* * * *

I hadn't known the Lord a long time, but we were becoming acquainted. At least that's how I looked at it from my end. He already knew me. I was in my Bible a lot, learning to know Him and learning important Bible verses. One was Romans 10:13: "Anyone who calls upon the name of the Lord will be saved." The King James Version says, "…shall be saved."

I knew that the verse meant saved from a life dominated by sin and its judgment—I had already learned that. What I didn't know was that it could have a little twist to it.

At the time, I was living in west Los Angeles. Nice. I had a grass-green (yuck) Volkswagen Beetle that was dented and scratched, but it had four wheels and took me around very well. I had considered getting it painted but I never got beyond thinking about it. With three kids and a mortgage payment, a pretty car was a low-priority budget item for us.

One day I turned off a busy thoroughfare into a residential area known as Brentwood. The street was lined with cars parked along the curb because parking spaces are rare in that part of town due to neighborhood apartment housing. The trouble with curbside parking is that it sometimes interferes with driver visibility. You guessed it. A *big* car lunged out of a driveway just ahead of me and ran into the rear passenger side of my Beetle.

Yup. Just like that—fine one moment and out of control the next. The car hit my back half on the passenger side with such force that my car spun to the right. In a flash I could tell I was headed up over the curb and straight into a light pole. Airborne! Dead-center collision coming up.

"Lord, save me!" I cried out, terrified.

Instantly, the words "anyone who calls upon the name of the Lord will be saved" flashed through my mind. I also remember thinking, "How bizarre!" Well, within seconds my car cleared the curb and landed. It didn't land up against the light pole I had been headed toward but it stopped in some shrubberies next to it. And the more amazing thing was how softly—yes, softly—I landed. No jarring, no bumps, no scrapes, no bruises. It was like landing on a pillow. I didn't see an angel, but I think God sent one to cushion me. I had called upon the name of the Lord and had been saved. His word has such surprises encompassed within the normal meaning of a text.

Delightful.

And, yes, my little Beetle received a new paint job—free.

It was a good thing I was getting to know Jesus personally because I had no idea how much I would need Him as time passed. I also had never imagined that He could fill me with such incredible joy, beyond what I could ask or think.

This excerpt is taken from my book, *The Tree of Faith, God Wants To Answer YOUR Prayer* (Ad at the front/back of book) which can be found on Amazon, https://www.amazon.com/dp/B093R7XQQJ/ref=cm_sw_em_r_mt_dp_NWHN2M1DZ4D6W0AZ5XEP

Also, you can watch my interview with Linda Olson on the Roku Channel on FTG (Fetch the Goodness) Network under *Wealth Through Stories* which promotes Kingdom Building for Christian Families. My story is featured in Season 2: Episode 1.

The book has many more stories from my life as well as an appendix addressing some of the significant questions often asked. At first, I had written the book to leave with my family and grandchildren but the more I thought about it, I knew it had a message that many others need to hear. Life can be tough, and we live in a time when we need answers, not only answers for here on earth but answers that will take us to live eternal life in heaven. My hope and prayer is that you will find many of those answers in the book, The Tree of Faith.

> "NOW is the time to LOOK to the Light, RENEW your faith, and EXPECT GOD to answer your prayers!"

Christine Schat, a UCLA graduate, and former owner of Fort Bragg Bakery. She loves to smile, laugh, and share her stories. Christine currently lives in Southern California but loves to travel the country visiting family and friends. She is especially fond of her grandchildren and has been nicknamed Gram-cracker. But her greatest joy is experiencing God answering prayers.

Chapter 2

Will You Give Up Everything For Me?

By Leena Ying Tang

"Hey, darling! Today I don't have to go to work so let's go to the hospital and have our baby boy!" My father's eyes twinkled at my beautiful mother. Long, dark hair framed her lovely face and, although young, she too was eager to meet their new baby. The year was 1966 and my parents were living in Beijing, China. My father was home on holiday, and they both knew their son would be considered extra-special if his birthday would fall on this particular day, October 1st, the Chinese National Independence Day. Eagerly they drove to the hospital, hoping that today was the day the baby would be born.

Yet it was not to be. The doctor told my mother that it wasn't time yet, so he sent her home. A few days later, however, in late afternoon, labor pains began and this time she was alone—her husband at work. She bravely took a bus to the hospital, unaccompanied, and after work my father and my sister met her there, anxious to celebrate the birth of the first son to the family. The eldest child, a little girl, had been born six years earlier and now the entire small gathering looked forward to adding a baby boy to their circle. Soon, in the early evening, the child was born.

"Congratulations!" the doctor exclaimed. "You have a beautiful, healthy baby girl!"

A baby girl?! My parents were stunned and disheartened. In China, a firstborn son was highly valued to carry on the family name, but I was a *girl!* Yes, I was the newborn baby, and my parents were bewildered. Apparently, the thought had never crossed their minds in the entire nine months of pregnancy that their second child might be female.

A week later my uncle came to visit. He was so excited to meet his new nephew, and when my parents informed him, I was a baby girl, he didn't believe them. He had to unfold the blanket and diaper to see that, indeed, I was his niece and not his nephew. Needless to say, he too was disappointed. For generations, our family had been comprised of mostly girls, and somehow our relatives had decided that my parent's baby was going to be the son for whom they had all hoped. Because boys are more highly valued than girls in the Chinese culture, my entire extended family was disappointed at my birth. Mother, before she was married, had dreamed of having two daughters named after birds, so she named my sister Yanzi, which means "swallow". When I was born, my mother wanted to name me Ying, which means "eagle". My father considered this. After all, the eagle is a strong, massive bird that soars through the skies with great majesty. So, he told my mother that he would agree to the name. Later in life, I would realize that my name indeed indicated something special.

Because my parents thought they were having a boy, my only toy was a wooden gun that my father made for me before I was born. As a child, I preferred playing in the mud, fighting pretend battles, running races, and climbing trees like other neighborhood boys. Although I didn't have dolls or tiaras, I do remember singing and jumping rope.

Even though I wore hand me down clothes from my sister and looked like a girl, on the inside I felt like a boy. When, I was in middle school, my female classmates were excused because they didn't participate in the Physical Education class during their "time of the month". On the other hand, even though I was in pain, I never missed a single class. One day I was asked bluntly by my teacher, "Do you not have a period?"

I responded, "Yes, I have a period, but why should I miss class?" My teacher was speechless in her surprise. Once again, I was acting like a boy, pushing through all discomfort.

When I was two or three years old, Mother dressed me as a boy. My clothing was so convincing that her co-workers thought it was quite lovely that my mother had both a boy and a girl. Ten years later, when I was eighteen years old, my sister and I went with my mother to the same company where my parents had once worked. Mother turned to introduce her two daughters to her co-workers and one woman blurted out. "No way! You have one girl and one boy!" No one could believe it, and they stared at me dumbfounded.

Finally, Mom humbly admitted, "No, I dressed her like a boy when she was growing up, but she really is a girl." I can still see the surprise in the eyes of those co-workers. My mother's secret was secret no more.

Although my parents treated me like a son, they did love me. I remember the inevitable conflicts with my sister. She had been taught how to clean, cook, serve, and do all the housework. However, I had been treated like a boy, so I was never taught to cook. When I came home from school, Mom would just send me to my room to study, excusing me from all household chores. Naturally, my sister was upset at the injustice, and she cried to our parents, "You always protect Leena and not me! You love her more than me. She doesn't have to do any housework like me. she's like your boy!" I could feel her anger, yet I could do nothing about it. Our roles had been fixed by our parents long ago and who was I to change that? Although I was five years younger than Yanzi, she was considered the weaker one while I, the supposed son, had become the stronger child, both in temperament and stature.

I accepted this position of dominance without complaint. In fact, I rarely thought about the idea that I had been raised as a son when I was clearly a daughter. The arrangement was simply something unique in our family and I didn't question it. However, I clearly remember an incident that happened on my first day of college. The teacher instructed the freshman class, "Boys on the left, girls on the right." That moment—*for the first time!*—I faltered in my thinking. I didn't know what to do. I stood frozen, not knowing which way to go. Finally, I go to the right. Suddenly, I realized how confused I was about my identity. I was a girl and had several girlfriends, but I also played with boys. Although I dressed like a girl, the word "tomboy" fit me well, almost too perfectly.

I knew I was a girl, of course, and I really did look like a girl, but inside I always wished I had been born a boy. After all, most leaders were boys, and I was always the leader wherever I went, from my preschool days all the way through my university days. Because I demonstrated positive leadership qualities early on and I came from Beijing, the capitol of China, I speak Mandarin well. My elementary teacher, Ms. Liang, who lived in Sichuan, another province, spoke Mandarin, but with an accent. Although students came to our school from all over China with their parents and spoke different languages. Mandarin is the government-designated language for the country. Ms. Liang trusted me and often asked me to assist her in class. The other students were even afraid of me somewhat because I had the authority of the teacher in her absence. When I was left in charge of the class, everyone remained quiet. If I left the classroom, the students quickly felt the freedom to jump and play but when I returned, everything quickly became quiet.

I enjoyed the authority I had at the school and simply saw myself as I imagined boys would think of themselves. My father held a high position in the company for which he worked, and he too was a strong leader, so perhaps I learned some leadership skills from him. Sometimes I would even look at the girls and say to myself, "What a shame they cannot do this or that." I simply didn't feel like I was one of them.

* * * *

Being raised as a boy affected my whole life. I did eventually marry, yet I really didn't know who I was. Because I wasn't trained as a girl, I didn't know how to be a wife and how to support my husband. The dominoes fell on top of one another as I realized I didn't know how to be a mother and teach our children. I certainly struggled in my relationship with my own mother, confused because I knew that she loved me so much and did so much for me. Yet I hated her somehow. Years later I would realize that the deep desire to reject her resulted because I simply didn't meet her expectation of being a boy. And, sadly, because I could not meet that expectation, I hated myself.

When I was forty years old, I heard God speak to me about my identity. When I realized who I was really created to be, I knew that the Creator of the universe really hadn't messed up after all. God had created me to be female, to be not only a girl, but a beautiful girl. That girl had grown into a beautiful woman, and I humbly acknowledged what I saw in the mirror. "I am a woman," I would say to my reflection. Day after day, year after year, I would look at that mirrored image and declare, "Leena, you are a woman." Soon I began to believe that I possessed femininity and I let my signature short hair grow long. I purchased high heels, dressed in colorful blouses and skirts, and learned to wear make-up. All this, of course, was foreign to me, like learning a strange language. Here I was, forty years old, just now experiencing what it was like to *think* like a woman. I wanted desperately for the outside of me to match the inside of me, the one whom God created.

Naturally, the tendency to think like a man showed up in my marriage. I wanted to be the head of the house like I had been taught to be. I didn't respect my husband, and I certainly didn't respect his role as a man. Inevitably, this distorted way of viewing the husband/wife relationship didn't work well, and so my first marriage failed.

And my second.

And my third.

Finally, I recognized I had been misled in my own thinking. In China more value is placed on following the cultural norms than on the identity of the child. A man is simply considered to be more important than a woman. When a male child is born, the family hosts a festive celebration. But when a female child is born, the family understands that the girl will grow up, marry, and thereafter belong to her husband's family. She will no longer belong to her family of origin. A grown woman could never work herself into a highly respected position in a company because a woman was expected to stay at home. If a wife delivers a baby boy, she is highly respected. If she delivers a girl, there may not be any celebration.

I once had a classmate who was from a poor family. She was the fifth child of eight, and all eight children were girls. Because the parents had so wanted a boy, they named each girl with the same middle name, changing only the first names. The daughters were Wish Brother, Loving Brother, Nice Brother and so forth. Finally, the ninth child was a boy. Without a boy, the family would be shamed by the community because only boys could carry on the family name, and shame was strong in the Chinese community, and so the parents kept having children until they had a son.

This way of viewing genders settled into my view of life too. I had always felt I was a somewhat anxious person, and I often wondered about the origin of my anxiety. The year I was born, 1966, was the beginning of the Chinese Cultural Revolution. For the next ten years, China would undergo tremendous change. The country was in turmoil, and so its citizens were in turmoil. My mother was expecting me during this time and, obviously, going through her own personal turmoil. I believe, then, that although I was not yet born, I still experienced her tears and sadness, her anxiety and anger, her fear of the uncertainty of her days.

Babies can genuinely hear and experience whatever the mother is experiencing. God created each of us, forming us in the womb, protecting us from the outside world. Yet even then, in an unborn state, we are still influenced by the voices around us and by the emotional state of our mothers. For this reason, how comforting it is to our babies that we speak kind and loving words to them. Reading and singing to children before they are born produce babies who calm easily when their mothers read and sing to them after birth.

Traditionally, strong cultural norms and values dictated the customs in China prior to my birth. The majority of women worked at home, cleaning and cooking and raising children. Only the husband could go to work at a business or in the field or in some other capacity to provide for his family. The man was always given the higher position because he was believed to be of greater value. After 1949, when China became a new and independent country, women gained more freedom and were allowed to enter the workforce.

* * * *

After I moved to the United States when I was twenty-eight, I was introduced to Jesus. Eventually I learned that God instructs us to respect our children and to acknowledge that they are gifts from Him, ideas that were foreign to me. While living in the US, I learned that most Americans love and respect their children, and I also discovered that children know more than we realize. This was not always how the Chinese viewed their children.

I heard of one Chinese family where the parents had given their children the best of everything. When the son was old enough, he moved to the United States to complete his college education. After graduating, he was expected to return to China. But the son had other ideas. In a conversation with his parents, he exploded in anger.

"I hate you! I hate you! For twenty years you kept me under your control and you forced me to learn this and that. I don't want to go back! I have graduated and now I want to work and do as I please." The parents were devastated.

Sadly, this is not an isolated incident. The majority of Chinese parents have extremely high academic expectations for their children which, if not carefully explained, are accompanied by a strong, unhealthy sense of insistence and control. Consequently, a young high school graduate typically goes to college only because his parents insist and not because of a personal decision to further his education. Naturally, this can cause great conflict as the college student matures, wanting to explore his own identity, while the parents expect conformity and loyalty to the family when the studies are completed. Genuine love and affection, of course, combined with healthy communication can bridge the gap between the expectations of both parents and child.

Through my struggle of searching for my identity, I finally came to a place in my life to accept not what I wanted and not what my parents wanted, but who God created me to be. The life-long struggle in search of my own identity brought me to a position of humbly surrendering to God and trusting Him, knowing that His ways were higher than mine. I may not understand much in life, but I do know that when I submitted to Him and accepted what He had for me, my life went so much more smoothly. Accepting His plan for my identity and for my life was the first step I took in letting go of fear.

Then God took me deeper into my story.

The year is 2020. The year of perfect vision. But that is not how things started out.

It wasn't long before the whole world was in a pandemic with Covid-19. It didn't seem real. We would watch it on the news and hear about all the case of illness and deaths.

It didn't seem real until a few months later. I came home from work, exhausted. Since I would be alone for dinner, I grabbed a quick bite to eat and lay down on the sofa. When my son, Raymond, came home, he said, "Why don't you sleep in your room?" I had no idea I had just slept for five hours. The next morning, I woke up with a fever and that continued for a week. Shortly afterward, I started coughing and was having a hard time breathing. My husband took me to the hospital where I stayed overnight as they started doing the testing. I was diagnosed with Covid-19 but they said, "Luckily, you are young, have no other disease so you can go home and rest. They instructed me to take my medicine, eat healthy, and get plenty of rest and spend some time in the sun.

For the next two weeks I remained in isolation. My two boys and my friend delivered food for me. But, there was no one to talk to but God. I had lots of time to think and began reviewing my life. I thought about how God had miraculously protected me at different times in my life and how much He loved me. And then God spoke to me very personally. Twenty years ago, He asked me three times, "**Will you give up everything for Me?**" I struggled with His question and finally said yes, but I knew it was a yes from my head, not from my heart. I was still holding back. During the last 20 years He continued to speak to me and draw me to Himself and I experienced many miracles, visions and dreams.

Now He asked me again, "**Will you give up everything for Me?**" I was alone and knew only Jesus could help me. If I died, I knew I couldn't carry anything with me. I didn't need to think about my response. It was a YES from the heart. I was willing to give up everything and follow Him no matter what.

I knew, NOW, was the time to tell my story. For some time, I wanted to share my story and leave a legacy for my sons. It was my way of thanking them for the many years of hardship and their constant support. Just like my sons graduated from High School, I felt like I graduated as a mother. My goal was to finish my book before Samuel's 18th birthday. But now, I knew my mission was much greater. So many people are hurting and living in fear and worry. But it doesn't have to be that way. God has provided a way to rise above the fear and worry so we can soar like an eagle. Over the years, God has carried me, protected me and shared His amazing love with me. And now, He wants you to know He will do the same for you.

Fully committing my life to Jesus was one of the best decisions I made. I discovered that when I fully surrendered my life to Him, He was waiting to give me a life of fulfillment and abundance that I had never imagined. I am learning to soar like an eagle.

If you too would like to learn to soar like an eagle, I invite you to join me on my journey *Soar Like An Eagle, Let Go of Fear and Worry to Embrace Hope & Strength* (Amazon.com) https://www.amazon.com/dp/B09863Y6JD/ref=cm_sw_em_r_mt_dp_5F6D8F6AJQ610T7XMWPK as I share how at a very young age even before I knew Jesus, He protected me from the fire, the flood, the explosion and earthquake. Looking back, I recognized His hand was on my life and He patiently waited for me to commit my life fully to Him.

Also, you can watch my interview with Linda Olson on the Roku Channel on FTG (Fetch the Goodness) Network under *Wealth Through Stories* which promotes Kingdom Building for Christian Families. My story is featured in Season 1: Episodes 2, 5, and 10 as well as Season 2: Episode 2.

Leena Ying Tang is married to the man of her dreams, a mother of 3 handsome sons, an author, speaker and an award-winning Realtor. Her greatest joy is for others to come to know Jesus and experience the freedom and joy they can experience in Him.

Chapter 3

How Can I Face Another Storm?

By Hatsuki Murata

The day was slightly warm, as if the sun had awakened and stretched its arms over the world to gently wake up the sleepy flowers, groggy with unusually heavy winter rains. I hugged my sweater more tightly around me, like I too was being beckoned awake. I shivered involuntarily.

I am Japanese. My family came to America when I was thirteen, nearly four decades ago. We are a quiet people, non-demonstrative but deep-feeling, and always appreciative of weather changes that bring lush greenery and colorful blossoms. This early afternoon, gazing at the expanse of the hills before me, I lingered, thinking of the generations before me who have respected the rhythmic cycle of the seasons. They would be pleased with the view.

Spring had just arrived in the high desert of southern California after a surprise bout of cold weather. Most years the mild spring season is short—only a few weeks, really, sometimes days—before the infamous scorching heat sets in, many days forcing the temperature into triple digits. We were accustomed to waking in the mornings ready to don summer shorts just days after putting away heavy coats and winter boots.

But this year was different. Because of the unexpected, repeated downpours, our local poppies were blooming profusely, and the spectacular view of the hillsides blanketed with bright orange flowers refreshed me as I stood taking it all in. Our poppy fields here are internationally known—when we have enough rain—and this year's flowering beauty had been dubbed with the newsworthy term of "superbloom". Ah, yes. Leave it to man to name something as wondrous as miles and miles of orange poppies sprinkled with gold yarrow and grape soda lupine "super-anything". I simply thought that God was having an immeasurable amount of fun painting the open fields this year. I marveled, knowing that these same hills so gloriously displaying their innate beauty today were only months ago looking mighty brown and barren during the winter. Who could know that the land looking nearly dead actually housed the hidden beginnings of wondrous blooms?

Where I come from and in my early childhood, along with teaching the traditions of the Japanese people, my grandfather spoke to me of something called kokoro. I learned about its existence the same way a child might learn about his tonsils or his appendix. "Kokoro is part of you," he told me quietly. "Kokoro *is* you. You must always listen to it." I remember nodding my head, hearing but too young to ask any questions. When Grandfather spoke, it was wise to listen. He said no more about it, and that was that. From then on, I simply assumed kokoro was in me, was with me. I treated it like I would an imaginary playmate, a constant companion who would talk to me anytime I liked.

We came to America when I was thirteen, and I found the move quite disruptive to my adolescent life. A young teenager trying to fit into another culture has much on her mind and my kokoro, like a toy outgrown, was forgotten, its voice dimmed by all the change swirling around me. It wasn't long in my turmoil before Grandfather suggested that I had forgotten my spiritual heart. So, I once again searched within myself, listening for the faint voice of kokoro. Once again, I found it.

Now, in my adulthood, I pay attention to kokoro often, honoring its nudges and whispered suggestions for my days. Today I gazed at the vastness of the view before me, and I heard kokoro urge me to be at peace.

The poppies brought another surprise to our desert communities: a rare—like once-in-a-lifetime rare—migration of painted lady butterflies. I have never seen them in the thirty-five years I have lived in the high desert valley. The lovely butterflies that resemble monarchs in color with their bright orange wings speckled with black and white dots did not keep only to the poppies in the fields on the outskirts of town. These lovely fluttering beauties visited the valley cities one day, swarming the local rose bushes, the neighborhood trees, and the flowering gardens. That morning I stood absolutely still in our backyard, barely blinking, and the butterflies flew all around me as I held my breath in wonder.

I inhaled deeply and held the life-giving oxygen for a moment, closing my eyes, before I exhaled slowly. This year I too held an inner excitement, something so faded I had thought it nearly gone. My kokoro was settling, calming, yet I could feel it push forward in my heart, wanting to declare a new brightness in my life. Just like the butterflies that seemed to come alive this year, something else was awakening in me as well. I've heard people refer to it a "season of manifestation", a time when something comes to the surface and shows itself. Surely that's what I needed, something to stir and come alive in me, something good and vibrant. My kokoro smiled.

A few days later I stood in my own little secret garden, my future shattered. I call it "the day of the butterflies" now, but then I had looked at the small area in our backyard with blurred vision. I had worked for years to coax lilac blooms to live under the hot desert sun, telling them in the morning that I would return to give them an evening drink, tying the midnight jasmine to the wooden posts that supported the patio cover. When winter temperatures dipped below freezing, I preserved the tender plants by either blanketing them with mulch or bringing the greenery inside to take its winter nap. My own hands had dug the holes, planted the trees, and worked the soil to welcome the flowers that came home with me from the nursery. This day the butterflies fluttered around me, their rare appearance countering the numbness I felt.

A storm had come upon me, the fiercest I have ever experienced, and I had yet to react.

Life is full of hard times, of course, and I had weathered many, as all of us do. Inwardly I boasted that I was well-practiced for life's stormy onslaughts, my inner strength and firm resolve ready for anything, and I felt quite prepared for a little "weather". But this storm hit with unexpected force, its thunder shaking my foundation and its lightning slicing across my days. My doctor had just informed me I had only one to five years left to live.

And, just like that, I was in the middle of the storm.

I had no time to batten down the hatches or gather my supplies. The waves were already swelling, rocking my boat from side to side, salty foam gagging me as I opened my mouth to shout my denial, my rejection, my declaration against such horrible news. Desperately I cried out for kokoro, but I could not hear for the crashing waves and the thunderous blasts in the sky.

Only two and a half months ago I had been in for a check-up, and in just fifteen minutes I found myself in nightmarish waters. I willed myself to listen to the doctor's directions—I was alone and needed to remember what to do next. *Go to the appointment desk, schedule this test immediately, then that test, and then that one. Return In four weeks for the results.* I mentally etched the instructions into my memory. And then I was dismissed, not unkindly, by the doctor.

The first waves of panic rose quickly so I immediately matched the swells with logic. I knew nothing for sure; these were only tests; no sense worrying about what could turn out to be nothing. With that, I forcefully shelved every concern, boxed every worry, and stowed away the jumbling thoughts. For thirty days, I went through the prescribed tests, none of which were pleasant and all of which were veiled in blurry shock. I did all I could to process the events. The tests were my nautical preparations, and I numbly obeyed the medical captain, mechanically going to appointments simply because those were my orders. And my kokoro was silent.

The ocean spray began to hurt like needles in the wind, and the moving water grew to be higher than my boat. These seas were rough, no denying it. A lump rose in my throat, and I recognized it bluntly as fear, the "what if's" of my situation churning in my belly, like a lovely meal gone bad. Every morning I looked at my emotional sails, flapping in the horrendous wind, and wondered if the mast of my mind could possibly hold the fabric taut, regretful of my previous boasting, unsure now of my nautical skills in the darkening storm.

A month later my physician, in his white coat with his neck-draped stethoscope, sat on the black stool across from me. I was sitting calmly on the examining table, my feet not quite reaching the footrest. He licked his lips and swallowed, and I knew instantly that the words he would say would not calm my raging sea. He somberly gave me the diagnosis: Stage 4 breast cancer. Spread to my lymph nodes and lung. Aggressive. Too late for chemotherapy, surgery, or radiation.

The doctor, great sympathy edging his voice, offered a pill therapy that may prolong my life, but he offered no guarantee. He looked into my eyes, kindly. "Maybe one to five years."

Unexpectedly, my heart went out to him in compassion, and I felt a momentary lull in the fury of the waves. This doctor was facing his own kind of storm, having to give his patient the worst of news. I asked him many questions that afternoon, gently collecting my thoughts to spare him additional pain, and he patiently answered each one. Within minutes, I summarized our conversation.

"I am facing death; what do I do now? Where do I go from here? I haven't had cancer before; what do I do next?" I spoke the words candidly. I wanted to understand it all, that minute, that instant. I wanted to know what tomorrow held, next week, next month. Would there really not be a next year? The questions flooded my mind, filling every nook andcranny of my brain, and I pushed kokoro to the back recesses; out of sight, out of mind.

The doctor stood, shook my hand, silent. He knew he had informed me as well as he could: I would need to find more answers elsewhere. He pressed his lips together, blinked, told me he was sorry, and left the small white examining room.

I was alone. Really alone.

In moments fear of death rolled in, heavy and menacing, a wave gaining speed and power to crest and crash over me in fury. I faced my own mortality in a millisecond—people die, really and truly die. Like most people, I had known that my life would meet this end sometime. Yet the future—*my* future— collapsed in a breath like a house of cards, and I looked at the sudden flatness of my days, my nights.

No longer is this someone else's disease. No more am I the one who calls to see how I can help. No more am I the one who extends her sympathy. Now I see that sympathy is not enough. Now I have empathy. Now I walk in their shoes. Now I am a statistic. My enemy lives in my house, a thief claiming that he owns the place. My thoughts race, and the wave swells. *What in the world can I do?* I cry inwardly. I am only fifty-one years old, and I have just been told that death may be coming far, far sooner than I had ever expected. The wave crests and falls mercilessly on me. In moments my thoughts shift to my family, my friends, and the loved one with whom I share my days. He and I have both been divorced, and we had decided that we would make a better life together. Fresh sorrow makes me gasp for air, but not at the thought of my leaving them. No, I could do that. But I nearly drown knowing the sadness they will feel at my leaving.

Suddenly I despaired: I will bring sadness to every person I love. Can I bear *that?* To bring this kind of sadness to them makes me wish I had never been born. I have a deep desire to just make my existence disappear into thin air. Perhaps no one will remember me.

I picked up my purse and made my way out of the doctor's office to my car. Emotions cascaded like a waterfall. I drove home, breathing purposefully, directing my lungs to expand and contract. I had to steady my rocking boat. Once home, I tossed my keys on the entry table and stood a moment, silent. So, this was it.

Or was it?

I waited, silent. I looked around, not seeing. More silence. I was unmoving. More waiting. I closed my eyes, still.

You are in a war.

Ah! I was strangely relieved. *Kokoro!*

I nodded my head. Yes, I was in a war. The enemy had raised its fist to me, taunting. Sneering. Sure of winning.

Slowly I came up for air. Like the dawn that chases the darkest of nights, the awareness arose that I was not yet without breath. I was facing a storm that threatened to take my life, true, and I knew that this would be a fight to the death. Either the cancer would be victorious, or I would be.

Standing there in the entryway of my home, I trembled with fear yet, I was aware that my kokoro was oddly calm. *Why isn't my kokoro stirred up?* I cocked my head, thinking. The numbness of the shock was wearing off.

I opened my eyes, listening now with new intensity. What *did* kokoro have to say? My thoughts shifted into questions.

Shall I continue with the book that I had been writing the past several months, the book about facing storms in life, and how kokoro can help a person face any storm with confidence? I unconsciously placed my hand over the pain in my left breast, and I wondered if I would be wise to continue writing. After all, how could I finish a book and still have time to go to doctor's appointments? If I stopped working, my income would drop and I would lose the money that I had been putting aside for the book. And will I even feel well enough to write? Will I have enough energy? The questions came in quick succession. Do I just forget about the book—just like that—and focus completely on my body? Perhaps I was not meant to write the book; perhaps it was all just a wild dream to write a book. Did I really want to spend every waking moment I had left to simply entertain myself to be happy?

And why wasn't my kokoro moved by any of this?

I sat down on the sofa in the living room, still silent. The questions had waned, yet I was still listening. My thoughts turned to my childhood, and I had one of those times when I saw my entire life in my mind's eye, like I was watching a movie in my memory. I settled back, the house empty. I turned off my phone. No interruptions. And I let the movie play.

* * * *

I was born in Tokyo, Japan. My parents owned a small restaurant and had felt pressured by my father's family to have children right away. In our culture, a firstborn son to carry on the family name is highly valued, and my father was the firstborn son. When my mother finally did conceive, my father's mother—my grandmother—went on a name-hunting spree for eight months, searching to find a suitable name. It must have the Japanese writing in kanji, the system of Japanese writing using Chinese characters of Tsune, meaning "always", with one more kanji that must have eight strokes. My grandmother, a retired Japanese language teacher, had high hopes that this firstborn child would take care of his extended family, as is our custom. What a surprise when I was born—the first girl on her side of the family! Grandmother had not even prepared for the possibility of a girl. I was born in August, the eighth month, so she told my parents, "Her name is Hazuki", the Japanese word for "August"—I'm guessing she spent just eight seconds thinking about this—and so it was. When I was about two years old, I mispronounced my name, saying, "Hatsuki." My grandmother did not correct me, so the name stuck.

Let me fast forward you past many of the storms I faced growing up, moving to the United States and getting married to an abuser.

One day I asked my boss at work what she thought I should do about the problems in my life. She was Japanese and had the loveliest smile. She was a Christian, and I asked her about the church she attended. She told me that she attended a Japanese Christian Church nearby and she gave me the address. The next week on my day off I took my mother to one of the Bible studies and we both became Christians. From that day on, my mother began "living in the light", and I was so happy to see her smile. All these painful things had all happened to us in the span of one year, and I had often wondered how I would ever make it through day by day, but there we were with a new life in front of us. My kokoro re-emerged, never having left, and I slowly began to smile again.

One day while shopping I saw a small red picture with a poem. The poem tile was "Footprints", and the words tell of two sets of footprints in the sand—one set belonging to Jesus, the other to a young believer. Then only one set of footprints appears and the believer asks Jesus where He went. The beloved Christ responds that the one set of footprints was when He was carrying his young friend. When I read that, I broke down and cried. My knees were shaking so much that I just sat down on the floor of the store, and my tears flowed down like Niagara Falls. I kept thanking God for carrying me through such hard times. For the first time in my life, the storm waves settled into gentle swells.

Over the years, the children adjusted to weekend visits, and my daughter came to live with me when she was nine years old. We did lots of girl things together, and we enjoyed ourselves. When she turned fourteen, she experienced numbness in her fingers and arms and was eventually diagnosed with Syrigomelia with Chiara Malformation 2. The condition, a birth defect where fluid goes down through the spine, caused nerve damage, and I blamed myself for her condition. She needed surgery as soon as possible, and she would not be able to finish school with her classmates. What bothered her most was giving up her dream to be part of the school ROTC program. But the surgery was successful and my daughter, even with limited motor skills with her fingers, finished high school and is currently attending college.

* * * *

My mug was empty, but still I sat. I leaned my head back and closed my eyes. The memories continued.

* * * *

After all three children grew up and moved out, I wanted to fulfill a dream to own my own little Japanese restaurant and bring back my mom's Japanese cooking. She could help, and we could accommodate her diabetic needs in a friendly and healthy way. My family was happy for us, but sadly the dream only lasted for three and a half years before I had to sell it. Being a first-time business owner, I had much to learn and, like my parents before me, I put all my waking hours and all of my money into the restaurant. When I closed the restaurant, I felt like a failure and thoughts of suicide returned. But this time I decided to face the reality of my situation, and soon someone simply walked into my restaurant on the last day of its operation and asked to buy it, and would I work for her? This was fantastic, and an obvious answer to prayer. This time the storm had looked dark in the skies, but it blew over. I was learning that I didn't have to be afraid of the weather; I was getting stronger in facing the storms. And kokoro was in me, beginning to have a voice again.

I started work in three months, the restaurant was doing well, and I was catching up on my bills a little at a time. I had no extra money, but I had my health and I thought everything would be alright. But I was excessively tired, and I excused the fatigue by telling myself I was simply no longer young. Money was tight when I owned the business, and I rarely saw a need to see a doctor. Then the skin on my left breast discolored, and I hesitated for a few months to seek medical attention. And now here I was, only fifty-one years old, and now facing cancer. I was both shocked and saddened. I had already experienced such a rough life, with so much pain. I felt like that had been enough pain, thank you, and I could simply let the cancer take over. I was tired of fighting. I had spoken as much to the doctor, and he had replied, "Don't you care about your family and loved ones? You can get treated, Suki, so go see the oncology doctor."

I set down the empty mug and took a deep breath, reliving the entire conversation.

This was terrible timing. After all, I was writing my first book and had planned to title it *Facing the Storm,* and it was still unfinished. Yet, here I was, facing a fierce storm—again! Questions thundered through my mind. *Is the world against me or what? Is it stress? Is it craziness? Why is this happening to me? Why cancer?* I searched for anything and anyone on whom I could place the blame for my current circumstances. I had worked hard, tried to be a good person, and after all that, this is what I get? I was fuming. I had been planning to pay my bills and then save for retirement so that I could have a nice, quiet life. I was planning to go places, see the sights, read, and write my book. Maybe do a little art. Facing death was scary and altogether out of place with my plans. Then the thought passed through my mind, morbid but rational. *Well, I will be with God, won't I? So I can go now—let the cancer kill me.*

But I was aware that my kokoro was quiet, and that confused me.

I stood and took the empty mug to the sink. I stared out the kitchen window at my lovely secret garden.

I thought about my life from every direction and when I could think of nothing else, my mind quieted.

And kokoro spoke. Here I am writing a book about facing the storm with a strong kokoro and I wasn't myself talking to kokoro.

So there in the kitchen I waited, staring at the blooming roses, the midnight jasmine. I took a deep breath, and told my kokoro, "I'm sorry I've been going through my thoughts by myself." Immediately, something inside me broke loose, like a dam letting water through. I bowed my head and continued speaking. "Kokoro, what am I going to do?"

My mind calmed; there was nothing more to think. I had exhausted every possible perspective of how to deal with this new crisis. Silent, I breathed. Inhale, exhale. Listen.

And there is was. *What do you want to do?*

I replied aloud, instantly and honestly. "I don't know anymore!"

Kokoro sweetly replied. *Choose death or life.*

Me: "I want to live but I don't know how I can."

Kokoro: *I didn't ask you to know how; I asked which you wanted—life or death?*

Me: "I choose life."

Kokoro: *Life it is.*

That was it.

That was all I needed to hear; that was all I needed to know. The storm I was facing was not the cancer: it was *the choice.* The act of choosing was the struggle, the fight, the storm. When I made my decision, peace moved back into my heart, shining like a full moon over a calm sea. I chose life, and kokoro acknowledged it.

I lifted my head and smiled at my garden. Everything I beheld there spoke of beauty, of an infinite rhythm and plan, of trust. Not a single rose worried about the wind or the rain and yet, what sweet fragrance it brought to the world, what velvety wonder it pronounced to all who listened.

This was the fight I have overcome: my unknown future. I have also decided to declare my stance, to tell all who will listen—my family, my loved one, my friends and readers—that we are not made to lose. We are not in a physical fight, one that can be easily seen and experienced. No, our fight is against negative emotions and thoughts that race through our heads.

I no longer waste time feeling sorry for myself. Instead, I focus on living my life one day at a time, sometimes one moment at a time, and making the most of it.

Now I fight with a smile.

I thought I was tired of fighting, but this time I love fighting; I fight with a smile.

If you are facing a storm, do not allow fear or negative emotions to control you. Be positive. Let nothing—absolutely nothing—take the joy out of your heart. Negative spirits hate it when we smile in the hardest times, so banish them with your beautiful smile.

For now and always, fight with a smile.

This is an excerpt from my book, *Facing the Storm with Kokoro; Find Strength for every Moment, Courage Under Fire, & Unspeakable Love When Trouble Comes.* If you would like to learn more about facing your storms I encourage you to pick up my book from Amazon.com https://www.amazon.com/dp/B093RQNJBX/ref=cm_sw_em_r_mt_dp_JQZH7TRGJ3AN3CBS1349

Also, you can watch my interview with Linda Olson on the Roku Channel on FTG (Fetch the Goodness) Network under *Wealth Through Stories* which promotes Kingdom Building for Christian Families. My story is featured in Season 1: 1, 3 and 6 and Season 2: Episode 3.

Hatsuki Murata, a celebrated author and artist, lives in the high desert of Southern California and enjoys her friends, her family, and her readers. She is determined to live life with a smile.

Chapter 4

The Power of Forgiveness

by Joanne Peters

"One more signature and the house is yours!" I said to the elderly couple on the other side of my desk. I was working as a sales manager for a development company that was building seventy-two homes on top of a beautiful hillside overlooking Paso Robles. My sales trailer was located at the bottom of the hill and I could hear the buzz of construction going on up near the home-sites, a sound that reminded me quite literally of the "movers and shakers" in life.

I was delighted with my work. The activities in the sales office kept me busy, and watching my clients pick and choose custom features for their future homes always gave me an inner satisfaction, especially when I was working with seniors. To me, having an older couple who had lived long, fulfilling lives still look to the future was both comforting and inspiring. I loved hearing the noise "up the hill", knowing that an entire new community would soon be forming, with neighbors meeting each other and children playing in the front yards.

This particular afternoon, I shuffled the documents on my desk and turned them around to face the couple. I smiled. "This is the final contract. Are you ready to purchase your forever home?"

Suddenly, a huge roar—greater than any noise I had ever heard in my life—sounded near us, growing louder with alarming speed. The husband stopped signing the document and, with pen in hand, looked up at me. The three of us exchanged glances and then turned to determine the origin of the sound. Before we could even turn our heads toward the window, we heard an enormous crash, felt a sudden lurch, and were thrown violently into the air. The husband went flying down the hallway, his wife close behind. I was catapulted over my desk with the speed of lightning. *What the heck just happened?*

The trailer, now tipped, was still and quiet, the air quickly filling with dust. I picked myself up off the floor, amazed that I wasn't hurt, and stumbled my way down the hall to my clients, who had also been knocked to the floor and were turning carefully to push themselves up onto their knees. We were all shaken, but alive. The trailer, however, tilted dangerously on its side and, when I turned around, I saw that a steam roller—the huge construction vehicle that flattens asphalt—was resting in our lobby. *How in the world...?!*

Turning back to the couple-now-become-fellow-survivors, I asked if they were hurt. "Not so much," he said, "but you might want to check on my wife." The woman, slower to rise from the slanted floor, nonetheless brushed herself off and straightened her dress as she stood.

"I'm okay," she said. "But I sure got knocked for a loop." Her wry smile spoke for all of us.

We stumbled to the front door, which surprisingly could still be opened, stepped outside, and soon heard the distant sound of a siren, realizing in moments that an ambulance was coming. Blessedly, all three of us were able to climb into the emergency vehicle with minimal assistance for the ride to the hospital. Talk about a way to build relationships with your customers! In the end, we sustained only a few bruises and came away with the story of a lifetime!

After that close call, I began to evaluate my life, looking backward in order to better pursue going forward. Questions bubbled to the surface of my mind. "What have I done in my life so far? What do I want to accomplish in the future? What can I do to make a difference today?" This questioning was the formal start to considering what kind of legacy I wanted to leave my own son. Looking backwards, however, brought sad and painful memories.

My father, a World War II army soldier tasked with the job of getting precious letters from home to his buddies on the front lines, considered marrying my mother, one of the best decisions of his life. Mom already had a daughter, Geri, when they met, but Dad welcomed them both into his life wholeheartedly. By the time I was born, Geri was fourteen years old.

I adored my older sister and, after she married and moved a short distance away, I loved going to her house after school to play with my niece and nephew. Mom and Dad, wise in their personal financial matters, had seen the devastation and confusion in a family when a will or trust had never been established, and adult children were left in a quandary as to their parents' wishes. So our parents delegated to Geri the power of attorney over them, set up health directives and other instructions, and had all the documents notarized. Later, when Geri and her husband moved to the east coast, I was a young adult responsibly building my own life, so Mom and Dad changed their instructions to list me as having the power of attorney since Geri was across the country. Everyone was fine with that arrangement and implementing the directives of the will seemed far away.

But then my strong and loving father, long after his retirement, had a stroke and was gone after only three days. Although heartbroken, Mom knew Dad had wanted his girls to have houses, so Mom now formally gave Geri and me each one of their investment properties. She was fulfilling Dad's wishes and continuing his legacy of care and concern for his family. Mom then moved into a retirement community herself and proceeded to enjoy her new life of golfing, traveling, and playing bingo.

Then one day, *Mom* had a stroke—one that took her ability to speak and write. The part of her brain that could communicate in any way, including nods of the head, simply no longer functioned properly. When she spoke, the words came out as gibberish. Soon she required fulltime care and could no longer continue to live at the retirement community. I was going through an unexpected divorce, needed a place to live with my teenage son, and Mom needed care. Seemed to me that the answer to everyone's dilemma was Mom's other rental property—her "ace in the hole", as she called it. My son, Jason, and I moved into the main house and we moved Mom into the attached studio apartment. Geri was fine with all the arrangements, and Jason and I adjusted to our new life that included nearly constant care of Granny.

Three years later, Mom died, and we were all heartbroken once again. Then I gathered myself together to settle her estate—pay medical bills, sell the time share, and disperse the inheritance. Then, one day a letter came to me in the mail with the return address of an attorney I didn't recognize. Quickly I opened the envelope and scanned the letter, then almost dropped it. My sister, Geri, was suing me for elderly financial abuse. Seems like she thought I had been taking advantage of Mom by living in her house rent-free.

I was stunned, not so much by the financial accusation, but by the fact that my own sister believed I had taken advantage of our mother in any way. What was worse, our attorneys didn't communicate to each other and recommended that Geri and I cease communication also—and that lasted for three years! I learned that, because I was the accused, I was responsible to prove my innocence while Geri, the accuser, simply waited. For me, that meant phone calls, letters, attorney fees, and appointments in addition to the emotional turmoil of the situation and my own work schedule.

Geri and her husband, Mike, had moved back to the west coast, into the second house on the property my Dad had gifted us, next to me. We seldom spoke, and I felt like I had lost my entire family. I had hoped that Jason would grow up knowing his aunt and uncle and cousins and that we would carry on the legacy of love that our parents had instilled in us. Now, my grief was only compounded whenever I saw them come and go from their house. I learned in the deposition that Geri had always resented taking care of me after school when

I was a girl. My sorrow deepened at the adult realization that my childhood dreams were built on falsehoods.

One day, I was taking the kitchen garbage out to the trash bin at the end of the driveway. As I lifted the lid and threw the garbage in, I began to cry. First my eyes watered, then the lump in my throat wouldn't go down and, finally, I threw down the lid and rested my head on my arms and sobbed. I had lost everything—Dad, Mom, Geri, my own household, and most of my money.

"God, where are You?" I cried out. "You were supposed to take care of us, but you took Dad, then Mom, and now Geri. What happened? I thought You cared!"

I hadn't thought much about God over the years. Dad had been a phenomenal father, and if that was what God was like, I was on board. Mom seemed to rally from grief after the death of her beloved, and I thought that Divine Providence must have helped her. But now, anything supernatural and spiritual evaded me. I had no peace, no assurance, and no one to help me with the despair I felt. I was alone, but for Jason, and I didn't know what to do. Yet the pain in my heart was incredible, and I broke.

My tears finally spent, I straightened up from crying on the trash bin, wiped my face and headed back to the kitchen. Glancing next door, I saw that Geri was feeding the chickens in their chicken coop. Impulsively, I cried out, "Hi, Geri!"

She didn't hear me. I cleared my throat and called again, this time louder. "Hi, Geri!" Startled, my sister looked up from the chickens and briefly waved to me before going back to her chores.

That was a pleasant surprise, of course. She hadn't acknowledged me in years. But I was rooted to my spot on the driveway. Something had happened *to me!* When I had called to Geri the second time, I felt a physical, tangible movement inside my body. Starting at my toes and progressing up through my legs, torso, and arms was a kind of fountain moving inside me. When it reached my head, I felt it burst through my hair and out into the atmosphere. When the feeling subsided, I felt completely cleansed, like I had been washed on the inside.

I stood in the middle of my driveway, shocked. The pain was gone! Literally. My heart no longer physically ached, the perpetual lump in my throat was gone, and the headache that had been a nearly-constant companion for so long had dissolved. Although I had felt distant from God for years, I knew intellectually that He, being God, nonetheless was near to me. Yet I had no idea that simply stepping out in one small action would be the catalyst to emotional healing for me. I had experienced an unexplainable, unexpected, unasked-for miracle.

I was astonished!

Slowly, I walked back to the house and went inside to sit in the recliner in the living room. *What had just happened?* I mentally reviewed everything in me, and I could find nothing there: no hurt, no resentment, no grief. All gone! In an instant! I had never before experienced anything so dramatic. **This is the power of true forgiveness**.

My heart burst open with sudden relief. *God cared!* He really cared! And He really cared about *me!* The shadows in my life were fading back into the light of sunrise again.

About twenty minutes later, with firm resolve, I took a white kitchen towel from its place on the oven door, walked out of the house and over to Geri and Mike who now were sitting on their front lawn, catching the late afternoon breeze.

I looked at Mike first, then Geri. Taking a deep breath, I spoke clearly. "I can't take this pain anymore." And I literally "threw in the towel", tossing it at their feet. "This lawsuit has halted my life. I want to live and love again. It's all yours. Take it."

I turned and walked back to my house, tremendously relieved at the closure I felt. In a matter of days, the lawsuit was settled. I had proven my innocence, and the estate was divided between us 50/50, according to Mom and Dad's wishes. Geri walked away with her inheritance, but my portion went to pay all the bills I had accrued to pay for the lawsuit. This is *not* what Mom and Dad had wanted for us.

The entire lawsuit wasn't fair, of course, and I went through so much trouble squaring it in my heart. However, I had recently read a verse in the Bible in Mark 11:26 (NASB): "But if you do not forgive, neither will your Father who is in heaven forgive your transgressions." I had recognized then that forgiveness was not an option and, at the trash bin, my pain pouring out to God, I had forgiven Geri. And, *at the same time*, God had forgiven me of my bitterness towards my sister. Throwing in the towel was my declaration to her that she was more important to me than the money.

Now, these many years later, I realized that my own lifestory mattered. I could forgive myself for the times I had messed up, I could share with others what I had learned, and I could leave a legacy to my son that I could be proud of. What had been incredibly painful for me could be used to help others when they went through difficult times.

Taking stock of my jobs over the years, I could see that I really enjoyed working with senior citizens. I'm sure watching my own mother and father navigate their golden years had something to do with that, but I also seemed to lean towards working with older people naturally. Because of my background in real estate, I decided to pursue becoming a Senior Real Estate specialist. Then I became a Senior Move manager, a chaplain, and then eventually was employed as a Community Relations director in a senior residential community. Building relationships with seniors and their families, counseling them on the timing of their moves, and helping them get past being overwhelmed were skills I loved developing. I often helped my clients when they faced the daunting tasks of packing up their things in a home filled with thirty years of treasures. We would work together to determine what to keep, what to give to others, what to donate, and what to throw away. I knew that, although downsizing was an important and necessary part of aging, it could also be an opportunity for seniors to reflect on the past, remember special moments, and be reminded of their many loved ones.

Now, over two decades past the accident of the trailer and the steam roller, I had learned that just because a person had a certain age number attached to his life, did not mean that the person was old or was to be forgotten. What I witnessed over the years was that, although the physical body ages and may slow down a bit, the love of life can stay in the heart forever. I found that, when I approached my seniors with that point of view, they were able to focus on this next chapter in their lives with anticipation instead of anxiety and depression.

Then COVID-19 hit in 2020, and I myself unexpectedly joined the ranks of the retired. This hadn't been my plan, and I was completely caught off-guard by the sudden hours that stretched out before me. The days dragged, I had no work to do, and Jason had graduated and moved into an apartment of his own. I was alone in my home, sheltering-in-place like everyone else, and within days realized that I was in a perfect position to review my life again and pray about my future. I discovered that my "setback" with Geri and the inheritance was really a "setup" for promotion in my life. The tools I had learned from going through that experience were the same tools that I would soon use in working with seniors professionally. I saw this as God revealing His purpose for my life.

Soon I was building my own platform to offer zoom workshops to help others during their senior years. Because I see these years as the greatest chapter in life, I primarily wanted seniors to know that reflecting on their lives was an important part of emotional healing. I wanted them to know that looking at family photos with someone sitting close by provided an opportunity for them to reminisce, to intentionally force to the surface the memories of special people and special moments.

Secondly, I also wanted to heighten the importance of having critical documents signed and notarized ahead of time so someone can speak on their behalf when they no longer could do so.

A third area I emphasized with my seniors was creating their own life stories for others to cherish after they were gone. Perhaps these would be written down on paper—the old-fashioned way—or even recorded digitally with newer technology. Children and grandchildren seem to know intuitively how to video-record and compile photo-books and I encouraged the intergenerational involvement.

The story about the trailer accident did not end there. Today I am the Community Relations Director for The Oaks at Paso Robles, a Westmont Living Retirement Community. This community is built on the exact location of the accident with the steam roller twenty-one years ago! My legacy has brought me back full circle!

Now I see that God was with me through all the shadows of my life, preparing me for my purpose today to help seniors. When I had lost almost everything, especially my heart, I was able to see how my sorrows were restored to gladness and forgiveness. The pains and suffering taught me that I can always have hope. Now I understand that it is my responsibility to make sure the next generation has the tools and values to go forward in life. More than anything, I want to pass on whenever I can that God has seen me through difficult times. After the forgiveness that He extended to me for my bitterness towards Geri, I explored faith in greater measure, learning that the Creator of the universe indeed cares about me personally. I learned that Jesus intentionally came to earth to live life like us, and that He died for our sins. The entire gospel story makes sense to me, and I want everyone to know that Jesus lives. As a reminder that God is always with me, I wear a cross necklace today that was given to me when I was six years old. The knowledge of an ever-present, personal God who loves us is the legacy I want to leave my own son.

We all will leave a legacy of some sort to our children and our children's children, and so we naturally want to leave the best of who we are. **The power of forgiveness is your true legacy.**

I'm constantly inspired by this quote by Mary Oliver, an American poet who was born in 1935. Her work, inspired by nature, stemmed from her lifelong passion for solitary walks in the outdoors.

*"Tell me, what is it you plan to do with
your one wild and precious life?"*

* * * *

Remember, a house is made from sticks and bricks, but your home is made with love. The place *you* call "home" is a place where you stay active by participating in activities that keep your mind sharp and your physical body limber. For more information on how to create the greatest chapter of your life, visit my website at www.centralcoastsenior.com to download a free worksheet on "Moving Mom & Dad". Please see Ad at the back of the book.

Also, you can watch my interview with Linda Olson on the Roku Channel on FTG (Fetch the Goodness) Network under *Wealth Through Stories* which promotes Kingdom Building for Christian Families. My story is featured in Season 1: Episodes 8, 9, and 12.

* * * *

Joanne Peters, a public speaker and life coach for senior living, empowers the older generation to embrace memories and find joy in living the greatest chapter of their lives in order to leave Intentional legacies that are without regret.

Chapter 5

Uniquely Yours

by Teresa Campbell

Being four years old may have been a very long time ago, but not only do I remember it like it was yesterday, I even remember the goals I had set for my future. Now, what four-year old already knows what they want in life? I did! My list was short, clear, and to the point and I was intent on getting it done. I wanted to be a Solid Gold dancer on that television program, I wanted to be an actress, and I wanted to be married. Everything else was optional, but these three were absolute musts. Collectively, these childhood dreams would prove to be a constant thread throughout my life that gave me something to hold on to when everything else seemed to fail. But I eventually learned that when we let go of what we think matters most, God moves heaven and earth to give us better than that.

I clearly remember the time that my family and I took a road trip to my Great Aunt Liza's house to celebrate Easter together. Nothing beats the combination of family, food, and festivities, but the stand-out moment for me was when my little four-year-old eyes beheld the beautiful and luxurious deep blue velvet curtains that my aunt had hanging from the ceiling all the way down to the living room floor. They reminded me of the backdrops that made way for the epic entrances of Hollywood stars onto the red carpet and, in my ever-so-dreamy imagination this was my time to shine! I had on my black, patent leather shoes and I was as ready as I could be. As far as I was concerned, those shoes were special, and they could create magic just like real tap shoes. Someone was already taking pictures and, when it was my turn, I jumped in front of those velvety soft drapes and struck my best pose like I was destined to be the black Shirley Temple. That's right, I had plans—big, big plans—that sparked a fire within me that day. With all my heart and soul, I just knew I was special and I believed no one could ever take that away.

Being black had never been an issue for me before, and I certainly had never given any real thought to the color of my skin. But when my mother had to drive me quite a distance to my new elementary school, I was one of the few black students enrolled. And, in more instances than not, I was the *only* black student in a classroom where everyone else was white. I felt like I lived in two separate worlds, and the adjustment was challenging. In my church world, everyone looked just like me, and I took a whole lot of comfort in that. My school world, however, threw me into culture shock and really messed with my identity. All kinds of questions I had never needed to ask started flooding my mind.

Why is my kinky hair stationary while theirs is blowing in the wind?

Why are my eyes solid black when theirs are sparkly blue?

My ideals about beauty had shifted and I no longer made the cut. And all the blonde-haired beauties saturating my TV definitely didn't help. "Wilona" from *Good Times,* "Vanessa" from *The Cosby Show* and "Sandra" from *227* were the black sitcom queens that I looked up to, helping me to hold my head high. But after a while, I was truly worn out by the isolation I felt at school. Goldie Hawn and Pamela Anderson with their light skin and blond, wavy hair became the new standard of beauty for me. How could I possibly live up to that? After all, I was a darker shade and my botched Jheri Curl hairstyle gave me *zero* curls and left me practically bald! The pride I once had in being who I was on the inside started to fade away and, unfortunately, that fire in my four-year-old heart was snuffed out pretty fast. I thought it was so engrained in my being that only hell or high water could pry it out. But culturally imbalanced environments don't fully embrace outsiders they are forced to let in. This was the place where I went from being confident in myself to being a "whole hot mess".

During this time another black girl enrolled in my elementary school and I hoped she would be my saving grace because I really needed someone to relate to. At first she was nice, but she switched on me—like Jekyll and Hyde—and started being really mean! Her language kept getting stronger and, although I did my best to ignore it, her behavior kept getting worse and worse toward me. Then came the threats that I was forced to keep secret because she said she would kill me if I told anyone. I couldn't imagine someone who looked *just like me* doing such a thing. I thought we would both find solace in our sisterhood since race issues plagued us both. But, nope, that didn't happen. She stayed on her mission to make me miserable. I wanted to give up, but instead I sucked it up which proved to be too much for me. Eight years old and fearing for my life—that's not how it's supposed to be.

I've blocked out many of those horrific times, but my mother reminds me that when I would come home from school, I would literally stop in the middle of the living room and fall to the floor—I couldn't even make it to my room, I would be so exhausted. That girl had put a mental whoopin' on me, and my mother didn't have any idea because she thought I was just tired. I didn't say anything to her, of course, because I thought it was my fight and mine alone, so I chose to suffer in silence.

But Mama caught on quick. She knew that my behavior wasn't the norm for me and so she took me to a therapist who determined without a shadow of a doubt that I was clinically depressed. Thank God for the wisdom that the doctor used to ask my mother to leave the room. Somehow that gave me the liberty to tell him the truth. I was being bullied and I no longer had to hide. The doctor then informed my mother of my situation.

Now my mother, being the kind of woman that she is, immediately made the necessary call to let my teacher know what was going on with this bullying student. The teacher then must have had a talk with the girl because, thereafter, she would be a little bit nicer to me. But it didn't last long. Everything she did was a trigger for me, and so I figured that it was time to come up with a new strategy.

And so I used my imagination. I found it quite a beautiful thing to dream up innocent, made-up scenes. But imagination can also be a double-edged sword when it is used to alter reality, and that is what I did. I used my young, pre-adolescent imagination to create a whole new world where I could be in control. I determined exactly what perfection looked like and then I inserted myself into that role. Being strong mattered too, so what did I do? I made a pact within myself that I would *never* fall under the pressure of the expectations of others. I was going to live life on *my* terms—nobody else's. It was a new day, baby! I was walking in my confidence again—if you could call it that.

When I started middle school, I had the chance to begin with a clean slate. I made new friends who were brown like me—except they all had heads full of luscious hair. But that was nothing my imagination couldn't fix because, remember, now *I'm perfect. I'm strong. I'm the bomb. I'm fine as wine! Who wouldn't want to be me?* And so I acted the way I imagined, and it worked—I made a few close friends that wanted to feel the same way.

The next step was to create a club for ourselves. This would be the ultimate way to be exclusively identified in our school, and so we called our club "The Passionate PYT's" which stood for "Pretty Young Things", and we had sweatshirts made to order. They were pink with black lettering and you couldn't tell me *nothin'!* I was all about, *I'm bad and I know it and I ain't too proud to show it!* I became the embodiment of that expression.

Then came the boys.

I was only about fourteen when I started telling them all kinds of made-up stories about my life, my age, and who I was trying to be. They all believed me, so I took it as a sign that my imagination was doing its job. Not only did I think not telling the truth was the norm, I thought it was justified.

Whenever it came to choosing boyfriends, I made certain that I picked the ones that I thought wouldn't reject me or cause me any hurt. They may not have been the cutest guys, but I did look for certain qualities. I would always try to find something special about them because that really mattered to me. And you best believe that I made it known that I was the ideal catch.

"I'm going to be an actor one day!"

"This small town ain't the place for me—I'm getting outta here to *be* somebody!" "Remember what I said!"

I dragged that story as far as I could and, when the relationship started to go stale, I packed up my story and my fairytale dreams and searched for a new escape. I said, "'Bye, boy!" countless times because escaping became my thing. I was addicted to the honeymoon stage of a relationship and couldn't get further than that. "I love you more today than yesterday" was a song lyric that I couldn't understand. Fading love was all I knew because it's all I ever had. That was fine with me and my altered reality. I was in imagination mode, so I took my new identity everywhere I went as I mastered my perfectionism.

To me, winning was everything. And no wonder—everything I touched turned to gold. When I was in high school, breaking records became a regular thing for me. Since my school population was predominantly white, it was a big deal that I was the first African-American girl to be crowned Miss Mauldin. Soon I entered the pageant world and took first place

STORY MATTERS

as Miss Black South Carolina and fourth place in Miss Black USA. Obviously, this meant that I was indeed beautiful—and I fell for all of it.

I spent the next five years floating through college mainly for one reason: to keep my commitment to my parents who said I had to go. But my acting dreams were eating at me, and I wanted to go to New York to spread my wings. I told my parents and, to my surprise, they gave me their blessing and didn't try to get in the way.

I was in the Big Apple for a year and a half, landing a few off-Broadway shows, sleeping on a mattress somewhere, working really hard. I figured I'd do what I had to do. I was still on the dating scene because I really believed a boyfriend made my picture complete. Becoming an actress and getting married were still my primary dreams.

New York didn't work out, but an opportunity did present itself to me to go to Los Angeles. All I had to do was pay a few thousand dollars to a talent agency and I would be sent out for all kinds of casting calls that would lead to my big break, or so I thought. So, why would I say no? Here was my chance to become a star in Hollywood! So I went for it.

When I arrived at the downtown Bonaventure Hotel, I thought, *Look, Mama! I made it!* But when things got rough and didn't work out, I had to toughen up a bit. *I don't need them! I can make it on my own!* This is how I handled rejection. Always looking for the easy route, I wouldn't really do all it took to make my dreams come true.

Background acting became my bread and butter and one day on one of my gigs, the assistant to a well-known director at the time started flirting with me on the set. Occasionally we would meet up and I thought it was a "relationship", but apparently it wasn't to him. I'll never forget one Mother's Day when he called me and was in a really bad mood.

When I answered the phone, we talked for a bit and then he said candidly, "I don't even know if you're a mother or not, but Happy Mother's Day, if you are.'

Excuse me? What kind of jerk are you to say something so insensitive? We had already had a conversation where I had told him I didn't have any children and apparently that important bit of news had gone by him. I had never been so disrespected and made to feel so bad. With the bit of dignity that I did have, I got away from him. And then I jumped into a relationship after that what was pretty much just as bad.

I had arrived in LA in January and by September a few personal areas in my life were going south so my mother decided to come visit me to give me some much-needed support. She wanted to visit a church while she was here and so I figured I might as well go too. We went to a Sunday morning service that ended up being an experience that I had never, ever had. I cried nonstop and had no idea why. *Is God making moves on my heart?* I wondered. When the pastor gave the altar call, I didn't hesitate to stand up. I went to the front of the church with both hands lifted up and rededicated my life to Christ. That awesome experience marked a new beginning for me—and I really needed it. I was all in and, even after my mother went back home, I continued to attend church.

I went to most of the Bible Studies and my hunger for God only grew. Meanwhile, my heart became somewhat unsettled because I was dating someone exclusively and, although I was still getting acting gigs, I wasn't comfortable with some of the scripts anymore. Some of the roles were compromising and I just wasn't feeling it. One day, I landed an audition for a movie whose director was looking for the next breakout star. And if I were to mention the director's name, you would definitely recognize it.

This is my chance to finally make it! What could possibly go wrong? I wondered.

But when I read the part, I couldn't see myself doing the things that were required. Not that I was even close to being the purest person in the world. But when it came to me and my public reputation, I needed to keep looking perfect.

Remember, I had always created a picture of what my perfect life would be. And now my career path and my spiritual path were going in different directions. I had to choose but, believe me, it was hard. In the end, I knew I had to do what I had to do and that was to listen to God. So I called my manager and broke my three-year contract—I had one year down and was contracted for two more, and I was looking really bad. She was upset, of course, and I understood that, but I had to get it out of my mind.

After that, I was set free and I was free indeed to find the true meaning of life.

* * * *

Part 2

Acting was the one thing I loved more than anything else and clearly that dream was coming to somewhat of a screeching halt. Having moved three thousand miles away from home with no backup plan, I felt totally lost. Letting go of acting was bad enough, but letting go of a relationship that I had no idea wasn't even worth holding onto was just too much. I knew God wanted me to make a clean break of it, but I stayed a little while longer anyhow. And that decision came with a hefty price tag, as disobeying the will of God always does. Finally, I saw the big picture and this is what it was: the Lord Himself wanted a true relationship with me. And then I realized that I desperately needed to have a real relationship with *Him*. I was used to saying and hearing "I love you" from my boyfriends but, honestly, I had never known what true love was all about. I didn't realize it back then, but God was showing me something about who He was and what real commitment was supposed to look like.

A guy breaking up with me before I could break up with him was just not the way it ordinarily went down in my well-controlled world, so the first time it happened, I was pretty shook. In fact, I was "tore up from the floor up"! In other words, I was in a really horrible mental place in every single way. Stripped from everything that reassured me of who I thought I was, I no longer had protective, self-built emotional walls. I was vulnerable and raw and had no idea how to rebuild myself again, and the imagination that used to serve me well didn't do a thing to help me now—I couldn't believe how God could fix my mess.

For the next five years I wandered through the wilderness. I was caught up in a cult for the first year and a half and, during that time, I slept on the floor of a one-bedroom apartment that was shared by ten people. I almost starved to death during that time because we were allowed to eat only four times a month. I was down to practically skin and bones and some people thought I had lost my mind. But that's what being stripped and broken looks like—being unhealthy on the inside ultimately shows itself on the outside.

Still, God had His hand on me. I frequently crossed paths with people who spoke of my great future, but I needed to get out of where I was. One day, my eyes were opened and I saw what God was showing me. I built up the strength and confidence in Him to one day just up and leave.

That same year in June, on Father's Day, I met Troy, and right away I knew he was an anointed man of God. After knowing each other for four short months, we became engaged and a month and a half later, we tied the knot! And our wedding was iconic!

Prior to us being married, I had not been with anyone for three years and my husband hadn't been with anyone for seven. I couldn't wrap my head around that time frame for him because he was a *fine* preacher-man! I had never seen someone so dedicated to God and I was incredibly inspired. But I didn't really know who I was myself, so I thought it would be a good idea to just stick with my husband's plans and purposes in life and simply take it from there. His calling to the ministry required a lot of time in church and it was during that time that I had to face myself and figure out who *I* was.

That first year, we lived in a one-bedroom apartment in Long Beach, California, and one particular morning I felt led to go to the bathroom, look in the mirror, and do something I had never done before: I had to face myself and say something.

My contact lenses were out, my hair was natural—no wigs and fluff to hide behind.

I stared at my image and took a breath. I did everything I could to truthfully say the phrase "you are beautiful", but the words just wouldn't come out. They simply stuck in my throat. I was in there for hours, struggling, but all I could do was cry. I was astonished at how hard this was! I yelled. I screamed. I moaned and groaned.

My husband heard me, but the door was locked so he knocked to get my attention. "What's wrong?! What's going on, baby?" he asked with real concern in his voice.

"I'm okay," I choked out. But I *wasn't* okay. A major transformation was going on, and I couldn't leave the bathroom until it was complete. Something *had* to change.

More moans, more groans.

Finally, after what seemed like hours, I pushed out the words. "You. Are. Beautiful."

Silence.

The fight was over. I opened the door, probably looking like I had seen a ghost or had gone through an exorcism! But I didn't care. I *had* gone through something—a renewing of my mind. I never before realized the power of words, and those specific words loosed something inside of me.

This marked the beginning of a brand-new journey for me, one that had plenty of twists and turns. I was still somewhat lost and had no idea just how much, but from that day I just kept moving forward. I knew that I was married to a powerful man, but I couldn't just latch on to *his* purpose in life. I had to find my own God-given dreams, and I trusted that God would show them to me one day.

My bathroom epiphany was incredible, truly changing the way I saw God and, of course, the way I saw myself. But because I had put all my trust solely in my husband to guide us in ministry, in time I became unhappy and dissatisfied. Soon I realized that I actually was getting jealous of him, and I was letting it get out of control. I thought at first that it was just about his complexion since he was a light-skinned black. I remember looking at his legs one time, thinking, "Wow! How blessed can you be!"

Colorism—the prejudice within our own race to discriminate against individuals with a dark skin tone—was having its way, and what did that say about me? We had a saying: "Black is whack, but white is right", and Troy was way closer to the latter. It didn't matter that he grew up in rough neighborhoods and that he had a hard life experience in Compton, California. He simply didn't have to put himself together like I did; people were naturally attracted to him "as-is". I knew I had gone from bad to worse when I became pregnant three years later and the only thing I worried about was the appearance of my child's skin and hair.

Then, when my grandmother met our newborn baby boy, the first words out of her mouth were, "He looks just like Teresa, and he sure did get her hair!" Talk about stabbing me through the heart! Can I be honest here? That was my worst nightmare come true—that our son would have my hair—and to think that I couldn't change it! But don't think I didn't try! I bought all kinds of products to smooth out my son's hair.

One day I finally realized nothing was wrong with his hair, but everything was wrong with me. I could keep going in this direction and be emotionally destructive to our son or I could pause and think this through. I didn't want my baby boy hating himself on account of what I was instilling in him. Several years passed while I examined the roots of my behavior.

I knew God had to go deeper in me the day I saw my little eight-year-old get sideswiped by that stupid arm-color test—when someone teased him about the color of his skin and he put out his arm.

"That's not my color!" he said defiantly. Unsettled and unable to intervene, I watched from a distance as he turned his palm up, exposing the underside of his forearm, the lighter side. "My color is *this* side!" he declared.

That scene was painful to watch because I knew that the desire to be lighter—that a lighter skin color was more attractive and more desirable—had been instilled by me.

Time for me to go to that mirror again! Once in the bathroom, I stood in front of the mirror exactly where I had stood before. But this time I talked to myself with determination, embracing all the beauty that my parents and God had given me.

"Teresa!" I proclaimed boldly. "Look at your cheeks—that jawline is beautiful! Your almond-shaped eyes are gorgeous. Look at your nose—you have your daddy's nose, and it's perfect just the way it is. Look at that dynamite smile! *That* will light up a room! And there's nothing wrong with those teeth of yours."

I raised my chin, stared at my reflection, and kept going. "You are quite unique! You are well-made with no mistakes. There is nothing wrong with you."

Then I added one more caution, with a smile. "Now there's nothing wrong with accessorizing—just don't go further than that."

Done. No more dismantling myself before bed and reassembling myself in the morning. I didn't need to do all of that to be loved and adored.

When I first started teaching acting to students in Lakewood, California, I truly believed I had to be hip in order to connect with them. Unfortunately, I used some of my old tactics of being something I was not and, when you're not authentic in being yourself, your true gifts don't get a chance to shine. But then I began to let God use me just the way I was and I began to see my true impact in the lives of my students. For all those years I had tried to fabricate so many unique qualities while all along I had these special gifts already inside me. My gift was acting, but it was limited without God. But with His assistance, I found myself and every part of who I was.

Today, I'm "in the zone" when I'm encouraging and uplifting other women. My heart leaps when I can sincerely love them and let them know that they were born for more. Through fashion, I help boost confidence and creativity in whoever desires to move forward in life. And through my business, I am blessed by God with a growing community of like-minded women. We honor women regularly on our blogs, and through social media we let them know we truly care. That's what I love most—shining light on other women!

I'm growing too, and I often think back to when I was that four-year-old girl posing in front of a camera. My child's mind could only see what the TV showed me, and so acting became the thing that pulled me in. But God pulled me even further! Who could have guessed that He would pull together my gifts in such a fulfilling way to bless me by serving others?

Finally, I knew. I was no longer my own. Now I could breathe my own prayer and mean it from the bottom of my heart.

"Father, thank you that I am uniquely yours."

* * * *

Teresa Campbell - Everything Teresa touches turns to gold. Her children's book, Tia and the Wonderful Land of Fab, is just one of the many gems birthed from her creative mind, and currently she is the proud owner of 1st Class Lady Boutique—an e-commerce retail clothing store specializing in high-end fashion for reasonable prices. In 2013, Teresa and her husband, Troy, were called by God to co-found The Secret Place Church in Pasadena, California, where Teresa serves as a pastor, worship leader, and the women's ministry leader for Women Helping Others Live Empowered (W.H.O.L.E.). When Teresa is not establishing her legacy by filling the planet with her awesome sense of humor, she enjoys watching Carol Burnett reruns, laughing with her friends, and curling up with a good book.

To become part of Teresa's growing community and to receive a free tool to guide you through the mirror experience, go to www.1stclassladyboutique.com.

Dear Ones —

it is my hope and prayer that my sweet Sydney's story blesses you as you journey on. Thank you for making your dash count. ♥

Live in Christ,
Victoria
John 9:1-3

Chapter 6

Sydney's Dash

By Victoria Chapin

The elevator doors chimed open—first floor, Mary Free Bed Rehabilitation Hospital, Grand Rapids. Inhaling with relief that I would not be walking these halls again for a while, I stepped into the hallway and walked toward the physical therapists' office, glancing briefly inside the open door. I stopped and smiled, hoping to express my appreciation, but my smile broke into laughter as I gazed at the white toilet-paper streamers draped from desk to desk, winding around the high-backed rolling chairs. The furniture looked like it had been tied together like a Christmas present.

"What happened to your desk, Glen?" I later asked one of Sydney's favorite therapists, remembering how gleefully I had papered houses in the middle of the night when I was a teenager.

Glen looked up, recognized me, and smiled. "Your daughter!" he exclaimed in mock exasperation. "She and Deb were apparently busy after hours last night!"

I nodded my understanding. "I heard they hatched a plan to 'thank' all of you for putting her through the hard work in therapy over the last couple of months. What a goodbye gift!" I knew full well that a toilet-papered desk was a high compliment. Sydney, our fourteen-year-old third-born, was going home today. She and Deb, her Child Life Specialist, had become fast friends, and Sydney had wanted to make sure that her therapists did not forget her.

Heading back to the pediatric floor, I greeted the familiar faces of the nursing staff and entered Sydney's room. Looking at my beautiful daughter, our eyes met and we grinned. I spoke first.

"Ready to go, Syd?"

* * * *

Sydney Elizabeth, our third daughter, had entered the world with beautiful, smiling eyes. She seemed perfect in every way until the doctors noticed two abnormalities that required further examination. Having previously birthed two healthy girls, I didn't expect my baby to be taken from me right away for testing. As her father, David, and I anxiously waited for answers, we prayed.

We were told that results from the tests wouldn't be available right away so we decided to go ahead and introduce our new baby girl to her two older sisters—Taryn, four years old, and Taylor, our twenty-month-old toddler. They were elated over the addition of their new sister!

When the test results came back, the medical staff told us that, although no action needed to be taken immediately, they nevertheless would recommend we make an appointment with specialists once we left the hospital. Sydney and I were discharged after three days and our family settled into the new routine that accompanies a newborn.

But Sydney cried more than my other girls had cried. Some days she fussed on and off throughout the entire day, and I checked every possible reason for her tears. Dave took turns with me when he wasn't working, rocking her and singing softly in her ear in an effort to soothe her pain—whatever the cause—so that I could give much-needed attention to Taryn and Taylor.

Trips to the doctor's office originally brought a generic diagnosis of colic, but that was ruled out after her six-month well-baby visit when the doctor detected a kind of "raspiness" in her breath that was thought to be due to a respiratory issue. Two months later at a follow-up visit, Sydney was still underdeveloped for being eight months old, and the circumference of her head measured proportionately larger than her body.

Dr. Murray spoke to me candidly. "I've called radiology at Butterworth Hospital, and I'd like you to take your daughter there immediately—I've ordered an ultrasound of the baby's head. They're expecting you."

I was stunned. My intuition had told me that something could be amiss with Sydney, but never had I suspected that anything serious was wrong. Since the pediatrician's office was located right across from the hospital, I quickly headed toward the pedestrian walkway that bridged the two buildings over the street.

What could be wrong with Sydney? My thoughts bounced around in my head as I put my leaden feet one after the other, hearing the mild roar of the cars passing under me, while I did everything I could to dodge the fear that kept charging like a bull at my every rational thought.

With my baby in my arms, I walked into the ultrasound room. The light was dim and I wasn't sure if the chill I felt was from the temperature of the room or the gloom that accompanies the unknown. When I was directed, I gently laid Sydney on her back and cooed my assurances, urging her to lie still while the tech moved the ultrasound wand all around her skull. Within minutes, everything was finished and I sat in the chair in the corner of the room with my precious baby in my lap, waiting for instruction.

The ultrasound tech quickly called for a specialist, and my inner alarm meter went up. *Why do we need a specialist?* When he arrived the two medical personnel looked at the film together, their backs to me, whispering. After what seemed like forever, they turned to face me.

The specialist spoke clearly but kindly. "Your daughter is hydrocephalic which means that she has water on the brain, but we aren't sure why."

I nodded, recognizing the diagnosis but unsure of what to do next. The doctor detected my unspoken question and briefly explained that an MRI would provide more information. He ordered it immediately and recommended that we have it done while still there in the radiation department.

And so we started on a medical journey we never wanted to take.

* * * *

The MRI indicated that Sydney had been born with four noncancerous lipomas—described as fatty tumors—on her brain and spinal cord. Although not life threatening, they were disabling and put pressure on those two areas. Doing nothing could result in increasing physical challenges as she grew, so surgery to improve her quality of life was the next medical step. Dave and I quickly made arrangements for the other two daughters to stay with family and we both gave blood should our baby girl lose too much during the surgery to come.

Sydney's first surgery to debulk the growths was scheduled the same week she was diagnosed and lasted eighteen hours from prep to recovery. A second surgery followed shortly afterward to insert a shunt that would keep the buildup of fluid off her brain, dispersing it through her body since Sydney's spinal fluid was not flowing normally. Biopsy reports indicated that the growths consisted of mature fat cells and were not expected to multiply.

But they did, rapidly.

Six months after the first surgery, to the doctors' complete surprise, the tumors had all grown back. Now Sydney was deemed "an unusual case" and the specialist in our hometown of Grand Rapids, Michigan, not seeing a case like hers before, supported our desire to get a second opinion. So, for the next several years we traveled back and forth to Illinois, while our daughter regularly saw a neurosurgeon at Children's Memorial Hospital in Chicago, having three more surgeries before her fifth birthday.

Sydney, optimistic spirit that she was, took it all gracefully. Having her vitals taken and seeing doctors became as commonplace for her as going to the park was for other preschoolers. She had weekly therapy sessions in our hometown to increase her neurological functions, and her therapists communicated her progress to the neurosurgeon at Children's Memorial in between visits. Sydney's many checkups and testing dates made the drive on US 94 to Chicago a favorite time to listen to Veggie Tales or Disney sing-alongs. Before leaving "the windy city", we'd stop and get one of Syd's favorite treats—either a giant chocolate chip cookie from the hospital gift shop or a big bag of cheese-and-caramel popcorn, also known as "The Garrett Mix", from Garrett Popcorn Shops. The long treks to the children's hospital continued until Sydney was in middle school, ceasing only when her surgeon retired and her Children's Special Health Care coverage no longer approved out-of-state care.

Sydney lived much of her life in and out of hospitals so the medical landscape became familiar to both of us. Felt through my adult senses, the sight of plastic IV bags and tubes, the dings of alarms and elevators, and the stale, antiseptic smell might have reflected the epitome of anxiety, fear, and despair—a place where joy and peace rarely showed themselves. But that was not the case with Sydney. To her, that landscape became almost her second home, and she instinctively welcomed every opportunity to interact pleasantly with everyone who saw her. By now Sydney, an outgoing eleven-year-old who suffered the loss of a normal childhood, had every right to complain, yet rarely did. I figured she had every reason to have a negative outlook on life, but she simply didn't see things that way.

Our family believed in Jesus so we based our lives on scriptural principles found in the Bible. We knew that Christ

Himself lived in us through the Holy Spirit. Our children were raised to love the same God who loved us. The gospel story made sense to Sydney so she viewed her situation from an eternal perspective, and we admired her for that.

Of course, we prayed for her healing constantly, remembering the times in Jesus' life on earth when He healed all who came to Him. As Sydney grew in age and understanding, she prayed for healing too, and we sought to live out our faith practically while we waited for her body to strengthen, expressing kindness and thankfulness to others as we served one another in love.

* * * *

Sydney just wanted to be like "all the other kids" and she fought hard to live life as normally as she could. But together we learned that *our* normal was different, filled with medical jargon and home therapy exercises, but also with Holy Spirit nudges, the same as in the lives of other Christians. We found that God often pointed us toward doors of opportunity—times when someone had no idea how to cope with the sad circumstances that led them to dealing with injury or illness. As Sydney and I became more aware that the love of God was seeing us through our own valley, we wanted desperately to share His peace with others who were panicked and despairing. Although we could not answer specific questions of *why* something happened to someone, we found that we increasingly relied on God's promise in Romans 8:28 (NIV): "And we know that in all things God works for the good of those who love him, who have been called according to his purpose." Our family definitely loved Him and knew we were called according to His purpose, and soon I sensed a specific anointing on Sydney's life as she embraced her situation to become a beautiful example of faith to those around her.

Sydney's perspective on life amazed me. I recalled how our daughter, even as a young girl, was aware of a bigger picture beyond the everyday, and her view of eternity gave her a kind of seriousness that was unusual for her age. Perhaps she picked up the idea by overhearing me tell her story to others, but I also detected something more profound. One day in particular, when she was just a child, she revealed her unusual perspective.

She was in kindergarten when her turn came up to be Student of the Week. Being this kind of VIP was a big deal, even with the parents, because everyone in the class walked over to a family-made poster that indicated parts of the student's life and unique personality. When Sydney and I were making her poster together, we talked about the prompts given to us by the teacher.

"Sydney," I said, "This question says, 'What is something you like about yourself?'" With a grin, I looked at my barely-five-year-old. She was already reading and would often say funny things to make people laugh, and I easily could have chosen a number of things that I liked about her.

She answered promptly. "I like that I have tumors."

What? I thought. *How could she like the things that caused her suffering?* But I kept my voice casual. "What do you mean, Syd?" I was honestly interested in her response.

"Well, I don't actually like that I have them," she clarified, "but I like that I can tell people about Jesus because of them."

Five years old, and she was teaching the world. She understood that her present circumstances, although uncomfortable to her, could be the way that God brought people across our path during doctor's visits and hospital stays. Intuitively, she knew that she would have opportunities to tell them that Jesus helps us get through it all.

Her pain and suffering became our own personal ministry. Before long, she and I would actively look for and find purpose in the headaches, the episodes when she fell down, the bouts of exhaustion. She willingly submitted to the nurses who took her blood and wheeled her to yet another MRI. I didn't understand it at the time, but now I realize that she had a rare view of eternity and so she didn't look at what she had to go through as completely bad.

One morning at home, when she was about six, we were doing devotions together. I read aloud James 1:2-3. "Consider it pure joy, my brothers and sisters, whenever you face trials of many kinds, because you know that the testing of your faith produces perseverance." I stopped, considering the tough application of those words to my life.

As we discussed the word "perseverance", we were led to Romans 5:3-5. I flipped the pages of my worn New International Version and read, "Not only so, but we also glory in our sufferings, because we know that suffering produces perseverance; perseverance, character; and character, hope. And hope does not put us to shame, because God's love has been poured out into our hearts through the Holy Spirit, who has been given to us."

I looked at my daughter, waited a moment, and then read the questions that were given in the devotional. I asked Sydney if she could think of a time when bad things had happened to her so that I could tie her suffering to the lesson.

She had been through so much. The year before, we had lost her daddy in an industrial accident, and her medical challenges had only increased. I really didn't think she would have trouble answering my question, and she didn't. But when she spoke, her answer was not what I had expected.

She pondered the question briefly and then said, "Well, there was that one time when my sisters almost dropped me out of the tree house."

I laughed. *That was what she remembered as a time that something bad had happened to her?* "Is that it?" I asked, expecting her to elaborate.

She nodded her head. "Yep!"

I shook *my* head in amazement. Obviously, she did NOT see any purpose in falling out of the treehouse!

Sadly, however, she would soon learn much more about purpose in her suffering.

* * * *

Sydney was in seventh grade in 2007 when her body started to quickly deteriorate, resulting in weakened legs and unsteady balance, and she often fell. Within months, she could no longer use the right side of her body and we brought in a wheelchair as her ability to walk diminished. Two additional surgeries to remove scar tissue from her brainstem and spinal cord, required extended stays at Mary Free Bed Rehabilitation Hospital in Grand Rapids, Michigan. Nevertheless, Sydney's faith had developed intensely over the years and she fiercely believed that God would heal her so she could walk again. Although these times were getting more challenging, she and I talked about the words the apostle Paul had written to the Philippians when he said, "…I have learned the secret of being content in any and every situation, whether well fed or hungry, whether living in plenty or in want. I can do all this through him who gives me strength" (Philippians 4:12-13 NIV).

And content she was through much of it.

* * * *

Sydney didn't want people to feel sorry for her. She wouldn't allow others to do something for her unless it was altogether impossible, and with some things she decided it would be just fine if she couldn't do them. Syd made up her mind that she would focus on the things she *could* do rather than on what she *couldn't* do. When the staff at Mary Free Bed encouraged us to make our home handicapped-accessible and to move her room to the main floor, our determined girl wanted none of it.

"First, Mom," she reasoned with me with adolescent logic, "I'm believing that God will heal me soon, so we don't have to go through all that work for the house when I won't need it for long. And, second," she continued, "I really love my room the way it is! I don't want to fuss with moving everything around."

"Okay," I responded, not knowing where she was going with this because she obviously had been thinking about the situation for a while.

"Mom," she said eagerly in a humble tone that meant she really didn't want to bother me. "If you don't mind giving me a piggyback ride *up* the stairs, then I'll work really hard to scoot on my butt, step to step, to get down!"

So that's what we did—every day, multiple times a day. She was so appreciative that I did that for her, that she tried to be patient with me in other things. Although no one would have argued that she had a right to be the center of attention, Sydney simply didn't make it all about her. She would do small things, like letting others in the family pick the radio station in the car, or deferring to one of us about where we would go to eat. On the whole, she pretty much put others first, stepping back herself. She surely didn't fuss about much and was intentionally grateful, gracious, and giving. Sydney made me smile often, and that itself brought her joy.

And with that kind of joy, we had fun—and lots of it. Even in our hospital stays, we became notorious for pushing boundaries because we figured, "Why not?" If our tactics didn't hurt anybody—like coming back from outings past curfew or sneaking visitors in past visiting hours—we gave it a go and simply acted like we had been given permission. And we never were kicked out!

One time Sydney was missing Spirit Week at school because of a hospital stay at Mary Free Bed, so we came up with the idea to have it there at the hospital. We asked our social worker if we could tell some people on our floor about it and they loved the idea. So we decided what the dress style would be for each day and we informed the others on the floor—patients and staff alike—that we would be celebrating. Soon the word spread and families of patients, wanting to cheer up their own loved ones with something that brought welcome diversion, joined in the fun by dressing for the occasion. Although Syd's room was on the pediatrics floor, she had her therapy with the adults downstairs. We certainly received a few confused looks when we went down to therapy each day that week in our Spirit Week garb, but we didn't care. Those who knew what we were up to, smiled, and joy spread in the halls in the midst of difficult circumstances, and we relished in that.

Sydney became known for her sense of humor, and the therapists absolutely loved her. Our girl, with her sweet tone, would draw in therapists—especially the men—and they would develop a kind rapport. Then Syd would let out her characteristic sarcasm, and I would get a chuckle out of the surprised reactions of many.

Although we tried to make the best of the trials, life was still hard. Some days I could barely get out of bed. I would *often* pray, "God, I can't do this anymore. She is hurting and my heart is breaking. Take this cup from us—it isn't fair!" And I wouldn't stop there. Bowing my head, I would go on. "Sydney thinks You're going to heal her so she can give testimony of Your healing power—and You aren't living up to Your end of the deal!"

I would be met with silence.

Other days, when I would go to her room alone to get something, I would look up to heaven and, knowing I served a God who could take my honesty, I'd shake my fists at Him challengingly and shout, "Come *on*!"

Watching her weakness and pain increase towards the end was almost more than I could bear. Sydney dealt with constant headaches, a result of the tumors, and when she slowly lost most of her functioning ability, the pain and suffering simply became continual. I watched her flinch, her furrowed brow above her closed eyes stabbing at my heart, and my own eyes dripped tears onto my daughter's hair as I stroked her face.

Then I would wipe my eyes with determination, pick up my Bible, and read to her—and we would be reoriented. The more we read, the more we learned—both of us—to abide in Christ, remembering His promises. He continued to be our strength. Much of the time, Sydney grasped that concept more accurately than I did, inspiring me, twenty-six years her senior, with how much she seemed to understand the purpose of suffering. Sometimes when I was with her, I received the distinct impression that she was almost chosen for this. I was reminded of Job and how he was set apart by God to endure so much suffering precisely because God knew in advance how Job would respond.

* * * *

The autumn just before her fifteenth birthday, Sydney's central nervous system started shutting down, and she lost all ability to breathe on her own. With breaking hearts, our family realized we would be saying goodbye, within days, to our precious girl. Although on one hand we had prepared for her death, on the other hand we had hoped that this time would never come, praying she would get out of bed, healed and perfectly healthy.

Now the time had arrived and we had to make decisions. We put her on life support to make her as comfortable as possible and, once we realized with certainty that her days were numbered on earth, we met with a representative from Gift of Life about donating her organs after she was gone. Although I had never had a conversation with Sydney about organ-donation, I didn't hesitate to support the idea. I just knew in my heart that if I was the mother of a child on the other end of this process—someone whose son or daughter would die unless they had a new organ or some other kind of tissue—I would hope someone would do that for us. I was absolutely certain that Sydney's spirit—who she *really* was—would live eternally in heaven where she would no longer need her physical body, so we donated tissue, arteries, several of her organs, and corneal tissue to help others.

The dreaded day came. Our family had determined that we would never say goodbye. We believed that our sweet girl's life would continue beyond the burial of her physical body and that she would be more alive than she had ever been. Sydney, breathing artificially through the respirator, simply slept. We talked with her directly, knowing that her spirit could hear us, and we once again assured her of our love.

I whispered to my beautiful girl as the tears rolled from my cheeks to hers. "It's okay, baby girl, you can go now." As I stroked her hair, I affirmed, "You don't have to hang on any longer for me, Boo." My lips gently touched her forehead. "You've done what you were here to do, so now you can be with your daddy…and your Jesus. Well done, my precious one."

* * * *

Around Thanksgiving, about a month after Sydney stepped into heaven, we received a letter from the staff at The Michigan Eye Bank. A young man from the east side of our state had received Sydney's corneal tissue. The note told us that he had been blind but, because of our family's generous gift, he could now see! This was our first family holiday without Syd, besides her birthday, and the ache in our hearts ran deep. The timing of this piece of mail was perfect for us. Although we cried in grief over the loss of our precious girl, we also cried tears of joy and thankfulness as her giving nature was still evident in our midst. Soon we received cards and letters from other recipients thanking us for their gifts, and I had the privilege to meet Carol, the woman who had received one of Sydney's kidneys. We've visited a few times in person, meeting her lovely family. Knowing that, in our loss, someone else was helped, has given us great comfort. After all, we are called to love, and what better way to love someone than to give them an improved or continued life?

Sydney had wanted to do two things to celebrate her fifteenth birthday—one, have a huge party with her many friends and, two, get a tattoo depicting her strong faith. After much thought, she decided that she would have the "Jesus Fish" put on her wrist or hand. This particular symbol, known in Christian circles as an *ichthus*, is taken from a Greek word with letters that stand for "Jesus Christ, son of God, savior". After Jesus' death and resurrection, believers had an "inside signal" to let each other know that they believed in the risen Christ. On meeting someone, a person would casually draw in the dirt with his foot a broad half-circle. To the person who didn't believe in the momentous resurrection, the foot-drawing in the dirt was simply idle movement. But to the believer, the drawing was an invitation to also declare faith in the risen Savior, and so he would draw a half-circle, intersecting the first arc, thereby making the simple sign of a fish, reminiscent of Jesus' telling Peter that He would make him a "fisher of men".

Both Sydney's birthday party and the tattoo had to be forfeited when a family member gently reminded us that, in all likelihood, Sydney wouldn't make it to her birthday. So Taryn promptly rose from her chair, fetched a black permanent marker and drew the "Jesus Fish" on Sydney's hand. At that moment, I decided that I would have an *icthus* tattooed on my wrist in honor of Sydney's desire, and her two older sisters and a few friends decided to join me. Now, many of us share what we call the "Sydney Tattoo". We decided to get 'inked' on Syd's birthday which fell on a Sunday that year. The tattoo artist, who usually closed his shop on the first day of the week, enjoyed hearing our story and opened his shop just for us, giving us a great discount. So, in the end, we ministered to the tattoo artist by telling him about Sydney's story, and he served us by giving us a way to honor both Sydney and Jesus.

We held a Celebration of Life service for our beloved Sydney soon after she died. We asked a friend to sing the song "Legacy" with lyrics by Nicole Nordeman that helped us ponder questions about life after death. Tears flowed freely as we each inwardly reflected, "How will people remember *me*?"

My heart ached, of course, wondering if Syd's journey through pain and suffering really did reflect to others God's love and mercy. Did her shortened life *really* bring glory to God so that someone's life here on earth was changed? And would God in heaven greet our beloved daughter with the words that resonated in our hearts, "Well done, good and faithful one"?

We think Sydney indeed heard those words when she entered heaven. Unbeknownst to us, her legacy had been written long before she was born, a plan that had been imagined by the Creator of the universe before He ever made the earth and the seas. God was the author of her unique narrative, to be sure, but Syd was able to understand it and live it out only because she stayed close to Him in order to fulfill it. She was young, but she had wisdom beyond her years. Looking back I realized there really is no "Junior Holy Spirit"—the same Holy Spirit that lives and moves in the lives of adults also actively lives and moves in children. Sydney leaned in and trusted, allowing a spiritual maturity and a heavenly-minded perspective that, even though she was part of the next generation, inspired her family and friends with her great faith.

Although we had been grieving to some extent since we had first learned of the tumors when she was a baby—I felt like I was floating in a cloud immediately after heaven and earth collided for Sydney. I knew we wouldn't see her for a time, and I told myself that this was not the end. But then the day came when I was to order the memorial stone that would mark her place in the cemetery. I had put off this decision because, in my mind, the act would make everything irrevocably final. Also, because Sydney had died when autumn was turning to winter, I had felt no need to hurry. Now the season had changed and I was considering what was to be etched on her stone. I dreaded even thinking about the topic, but one spring day I woke up and just knew it was time. I often wonder if it was the Holy Spirit nudging me because I was in a good place spiritually by then. I called and made an appointment to do it on my lunch hour that day. The morning dragged on for hours and finally it was time to go. On the way to the appointment, I remembered what my pastor had said to me one time when he visited us at the hospital. We had been telling him that we were getting Sydney's tattoo on her birthday because she wasn't able to get it herself. With a smile, our pastor said, "You know, you could have her tattoo etched on her memorial stone…"

Immediately, my mind went to "the dash", that small written line that bridges the date that someone was born and the date someone died. Often used in sermons and eulogies, the idea comes from a poem "The Dash Between the Dates" by Lucille Britt, and reminds us to consider carefully the "dash" in our own lives.

My heart skipped a beat. *That's it!* We would place the *ichthus* on her marker between her earthly and eternal birthdays, the Jesus Fish to symbolize all the life in between. Sydney would indeed get her tattoo, and her legacy would also be tattooed on the hearts of many. That was all I needed to know to complete in my heart the full circle of Sydney's life. Full to the brim with the reality of God covering her pain and suffering, my daughter had found early in life the true meaning of her days. She moved from each sunrise to every sunset trusting in the One who had created her. She loved Him and trusted Him completely. With that deep knowledge in her soul, the suffering in her body paled in comparison, and she was eager to spread the faithfulness of her God to all who would listen.

I knew without a doubt what "the dash" represented for my daughter.

Sydney's dash meant Jesus.

* * * *

Victoria Chapin—chaplain, speaker, and award-winning author of Undaunted: A Prayer Journal—*inspires others to find hope and healing in Jesus through grief support, women's ministries and the creative arts. She is passionate about joy and embraces the truth that Jesus came so that we would have life in abundance (John 10:10). She serves as co-director for The Well Ministry for Creatives, is a mom to twelve and "grammy" to thirteen, and lives in Zeeland, MI, with her husband, Jim. She loves everything coffee, especially when it's shared with friends. To read more about Sydney's life, watch for Victoria's book This Happened...so the Signs, Wonders, and Miracles of God Can Be Seen. For more encouragement from Victoria, you can hear her story on ROKU. Just go to FTG Network (Fetch the Goodness) and click on Wealth Through Stories, Season 2: Episodes 7, 8 & 9. She would also love to connect with you at* www.victoriachapin.com.

Chapter 7

His Ways Are Higher

By Linda A. Olson

Mom, standing in the entryway of our 1959 farmhouse, her breakfast apron speckled with breadcrumbs from making our sandwiches, waved as we boarded the bus. "Don't forget! As soon as you come home from school, change your clothes and help with the potatoes." Her shouts barely reached our ears before the bus door unfolded to close out the crisp morning chill. Violet, Leonard, Vera, and I hurriedly settled onto the green vinyl bench seats just moments before the gas engine lurched us forward.

Fall harvest was in full swing. Our family of seven knew firsthand about "if you don't work, you don't eat" and we didn't complain. Cracking open a steaming baked potato in the dead of winter was reward enough for our labors. Nodding my head briefly to Mom through the bus window, I settled into my own world for the hour-long ride.

I thought of the school I had attended last year. The imitation red-brick building had sheltered my father while he mastered his sums and learned the alphabet. For eight years, in the same one-room schoolhouse, I had recited poetry and drawn maps of foreign countries, happily studying with thirty other children who lived in our small Canadian community. The hardwood desks, arranged by grade, were the academic nests of friends and family. Our distant neighbor Herb, my step-uncle Walter, and I all had wrapped our growing adolescent frames around the chairs in the coveted well-lit area next to the windows of the schoolroom, the place reserved for eighth graders.

Now the country schools had consolidated, and students rode a bus into town to gain the benefits of more formal education. Although I could hardly complain about getting a ride—trudging through fifteen inches of snow for three-quarters of a mile in forty-degree-below-zero weather was not my idea of fun—getting up before dawn to ride the bus an hour every morning meant an hour's ride every night only to arrive home at twilight. The Bergen children, as we were known, were the first to board the bus and the last to leave.

Now those days were behind me, and I was growing up—much faster than I wanted, to be sure. Meager attempts at finding my identity blurred among seventy-five freshmen classmates. Our high school student body topped out at two hundred fifty pupils—hardly the cozy, intimate circle of friends that I had hoped would welcome a local farm girl.

After the day's lessons and the long ride home, I hopped down the steps of the bus and lugged my book bag to my bedroom. I changed clothes—work in the garden required well-worn denim jeans and a hand-me-down loose, long-sleeved cotton shirt—and stopped in the kitchen to quickly make a peanut butter-and-jelly sandwich. Tossing the dirty knife into the dishpan, I hurried to the garden to join the others.

Over one hundred sixty acres surrounded our three-bedroom farmhouse. We must have looked like a bullseye from the air, with our property being surrounded by towering trees, cultivated fields, and a country road. Our vegetable garden lay northwest of the front of the house, a bit of an unusual location but one that caught the necessary six hours of afternoon sunlight. Taking a bite of my sandwich, I pushed open the front screen door with my foot and saw that Mom had recruited some extra help for the day's task. Grandma, on crutches but eager to help, and Grandpa Warkentin along with Aunt Laurie nodded their greetings. Three-year-old Karen, Aunt Laurie's older daughter, played with my little brother. Billy was two years old and melted everyone's heart with his bib overalls, bare feet, and winsome smile. He tagged along everywhere, always wanting to be part of the action. Today that action would include burrowing beneath the wilted potato leaves in our Manitoban soil to dig out the Red Russet and Golden Yukon potatoes which would be stored in the basement for the winter.

Mom looked out across the front field, her hand shielding her eyes from the late afternoon sun. She spoke quietly, within earshot of Grandpa. "Last year we took so many trips with the pails; today we'll use the front-loader to bring the potatoes right up to the front step, as close as we can get to the house."

Grandpa nodded, and Mom glanced my way. She must have seen the question in my eyes. My ears had perked up at the overheard suggestion and I was mutely anticipating her next words. Remembering how my arms had ached last year after hauling two five-gallon pails full of potatoes for hours, I would dearly love to avoid the myriad trips from the garden to the basement in the late-September heat.

"Would you like to drive, Linda?"

I broke into a smile. At only fourteen, I was already an old hand at driving the Cockshutt 35 tractor. Taking a turn driving large farm equipment was a common responsibility for most teenagers in the area, bridging the gap between childhood chores and essential farming tasks on the family homestead.

Mom continued her instructions. "We'll pile the potatoes in the front-end loader. When it's full, Linda, drive it to the front of the house. Then we'll unload it with the pails and carry the potatoes to the basement."

She didn't need to repeat her words. I nodded my obedience and quickly ran to climb the thirty-four-inch tire, boosting myself into the red metal seat. I could already taste the dust flying in the autumn air, envisioning the tractor bouncing its way along the well-worn path to the house.

* * * *

I parked the tractor near the garden where I joined Grandpa, Mom, Violet, and Vera. We emptied pail after pail of potatoes into the bucket of the front-end loader until it could hold no more without spilling. Now it was time to head back to the house. Hopping once again into the metal seat, I positioned myself behind the wheel and turned the key. I peered over the top of the faded yellow tractor and, carefully shifting into reverse, backed the vehicle away from the garden, turning the steering wheel to change directions. Next, I shifted into drive and steered the 5,000 pound tractor toward the doorway of our pink stucco farmhouse. Billy and Karen played on the front step, watching my approach.

I neared the house and released the hand throttle, one foot on the clutch and the other on the brake. *This was so much easier than toting heavy pails*, I thought. *We'll be finished in no time.* I pressed the brake, anticipating the deceleration of the Cockshutt.

It didn't happen.

The tractor didn't slow, didn't obey my command to slow its pace.

I gripped the steering wheel for leverage and pressed harder on the brake. The huge machine refused to slow. Alarmed, I realized the house was rushing up too quickly. I gathered all my strength, slid off the seat to a standing position and, with all my weight, jammed my foot on the brake, pumping up and down, up and down, demanding that the wheels stop their turning.

No response.

Bewildered and confused, I sensed the betrayal of the machine beneath me, rejecting my efforts to bring it under control. Quickly it was swallowing the distance to the house. I locked eyes with Mom, silently pleading for split-second direction; all I saw was my own panic reflected in her eyes. I screamed the only explanation I knew.

"I can't stop the tractor!"

I kept jumping on the brake. The tractor aimed for the house as if it was an arrow headed for its mark. I stomped on the brake, the clutch, then the brake again. Nothing. I turned my head slightly to catch any sound of Mom telling me what to do, but all I could hear was the engine growling its refusal to halt.

I could see that Mom was screaming now, but I couldn't make out her words. I put all my weight on the steering wheel and lifted myself up slightly and came down hard on the brake with all the force I could muster. *Oh, God, what do I do? The house is close—too close. I can't stop the tractor, Mom! I can't stop...!*

Mom shrieked as the front-end loader slammed into the stucco wall of the house and white wooden doorframe. The impact threw me forward into the steering wheel. I straightened my body and heard the horrific sounds of splitting wood as the doorframe dismantled. But, the kids! *Where were the kids? Where was Billy?*

The tractor had slammed into the house exactly where Karen and Billy stood. Billy, attempting to escape the huge machine that was barreling toward him, had taken one step in front of the stucco house, almost as if to mark his destiny.

The machine, its angry rumble still spitting fury, had halted its impulsive rampage just inside the double door. Through the swirling furry I saw Karen's colorful floral blouse wedged between the splintered panels. Quiet whimpering told me she was alive—*thank God!*—and I strained to hear Billy's little-boy sobs. But I could hear only Mom screaming above the noise of the engine. And this time I could make out her words.

"My son is dying! My son is dying!"

My eyes swept the scene wildly, looking for the baby brother who giggled and chased fireflies. My heart cried the words my lips could not form.

Where was Billy?

Mom, in three steps, sprang toward me and vaulted up the Cockshott. Landing beside me, she jerked the gear shift into reverse, and forced the family-friend-turned-enemy to back away from its prey. Then she yanked the key and killed the engine of the mad beast. We leapt off its back simultaneously and, seeing what we didn't want to see, ran to the crumpled overall-clad form on the concrete step.

Billy.

* * * *

My brain shifted into auto-pilot. Get Billy. *Get Billy!*

I ran to the limp figure that only moments before had been playing with a bug on the porch with Karen. Grandpa frantically threw the broken boards of the front doors behind them as Aunt Laurie grabbed little Karen. Out of the corner of my eye I saw Mom hurdle the rubble to what had been the entry to the house. A moment later she leapt over the shattered doorframe—now empty of sheltering Karen—and bolted to the silver-grey Ford sedan parked in the garage, car keys in hand.

Scooping up Billy, I wrapped one arm under, one arm over the too-still shoulders, the same way I had held him as a newborn. His semi-conscious form molded easily into my body as I spun around with him to race after Mom to the car. Vera was close behind.

I noticed that Billy's face bore the smudge marks of a little-boy swipe at a runny nose. Instinctively I knew who would go and who would stay. Violet would hold down the fort, preparing supper while delegating evening chores to Leonard when he returned from the field. Busy hands had always been

Violet's way of helping in a crisis. Aunt Laurie would drive Grandma, Grandpa, and Karen to the hospital while stopping for a moment to pick up Uncle George.

* * * *

And Billy. *Billy!*

Even as I cradled his semi-conscious form in one arm and grabbed the door handle of the Ford with the other, I could not comprehend his injuries. Accidents were common in farming communities, and I knew that in the midst of an emergency, hands moved while hearts prayed. But now my head also pounded with slicing questions. *Why wouldn't the tractor stop? Did I do something wrong? Why didn't I turn the wheel harder? Why did this happen? Billy isn't really hurt badly, is he? Why didn't that tractor stop?*

* * * *

Dad stared forward, his gaze never wavering from the narrow gravel road. His calloused hands gripped the ebony steering wheel as they always did—fingers on top, thumbs below. Now I could see those thumbs and fingers moving back and forth around the circle, clenching into fists. His eyes darted from road to rearview mirror to side mirror to the road again. Mom, turning on the blue vinyl seat to see Billy better, spoke quietly to Dad, her quavering voice summarizing what had happened. Dad's response was clipped.

"Nothing wrong with those brakes."

It was a sentence that would haunt me for years. Although Dad would never blame me directly for the accident, his words underscored my own frantic search for the reason that caused the little boy who lay in my arms to become weaker as the color drained from his rosy little cheeks.

The speedometer on the 1962 Ford approached ninety. Silence reigned in the car, forcing itself on us as an unspoken command. I cradled Billy in my trembling arms in the back seat as the countryside rushed past. The triangular window at my right shoulder snapped images of harvesters on neighboring farms. Everyday life. Now everyday life was shattered.

Vera looked over at me. At eight years of age, my younger sister was as fun-loving as she was hard-working. Now her mouth quivered in an effort to keep back sobs that would distract Dad, her shaking hand awkwardly stroking Billy's tousled goldenrod hair. I returned her glance, and nodded. There was nothing to say; my mouth wouldn't form any words.

Billy's cornflower-blue eyes fluttered open and focused on mine.

"Owee, Nina. Owee." He gently moved his legs, as if trying to run away from the pain. I winced at his nickname for me.

I tightened my arms around him and refused to take my eyes off his face. Before I could form any words of comfort to him, Billy's eyes rolled back.

His body went limp.

* * * *

Dad swung the Ford up to the emergency entrance of the hospital parking lot. Mom jumped out of the car just as it stopped, ran around the front, and jerked open my door. The cool autumn air rushed in as she scooped Billy from my arms and turned and ran into the hospital. Billy, though unconscious, looked fine; no blood stained his little body, no bruise or scrape belied an injury. My mind fought with my heart. Surely he would be alright. Dad quickly unfolded his tall frame from the car and directed his words to Vera and me.

"Wait here," he commanded.

Then he turned to catch up to Mom.

Mutely nodding, we watched as the double doors swallowed Mom, Dad, and Billy. Although we remained in the car, I felt my heart go right through those double doors with them. I felt hollow inside.

A long time passed.

Vera and I watched the cars come and go in the parking lot, shifting our position in the back seat of the car. We didn't speak; we simply wouldn't—or couldn't—allow the questions in our minds to form themselves into words.

I glanced out the window again. This time I saw the '52 Plymouth wagon belonging to my aunt and uncle pull up next to us. When they parked and opened the car door, I heard little Karen whimpering softly in Aunt Laurie's arms. Wordless, they tumbled awkwardly out of the car and hurried to the hospital entrance where they too were swallowed by the double doors.

Then we cried. And cried and cried.

And we waited. And waited and waited.

Doctors' offices and hospitals and emergency rooms represented a completely foreign culture to us. We had no idea what was going on behind those double doors or how long it would take. Our parents, expecting us to obey without question and to do so until further notice, knew where we were and we knew they would return to us when they could. Until then my younger sister and I, holding hands and weeping, now begged God repeatedly, "Whatever you do, God, don't let Billy die."

But God did not answer my prayer the way I had hoped. That night Billy went to be with Jesus. Some days I could barely put one foot in front of the other because of grief and sorrow.

But slowly—some days ever so slowly—I began to put one foot in front of the other with more confidence, with a greater understanding of life. Instead of simply wishing my pain would go away, I discovered forgiveness is a choice. I could choose transformation. I could choose to walk *through* my grief-based pain with forgiveness and, more specifically, self-forgiveness.

My walk of horrific pain and guilt ultimately led me to enjoy a life I never knew was possible. Over many years and a deep faith in God, I found strength and courage to face every challenge, every fear, every frustration that stood in my way. I had many questions, and eventually, only one answer. The scripture verses found in Isaiah became my lifeline:

> *For My thoughts are not your thoughts, Nor are your ways My ways, says the LORD.*
> *For as the heavens are higher than the earth, So are My ways higher than your ways, And My thoughts than your thoughts.*
>
> Isaiah 55:8,9 (NKJV)

I came to believe that although there are many things on earth I may not understand, when I could fully trust that, *His Ways Are Higher,* life became a whole lot simpler.

* * * *

Many years later, after coming to complete healing and grasping the power of story, I was given a new mission, "*To Impact A Million People a Year Through Story.*" Although, I didn't have a clue where to start, I said, "Yes". In less than six years God led me step by step and I began sharing my story to thousands, no, millions of people through podcasts, newspapers, magazines, radio and National T.V. And then I knew this was only the beginning. It wasn't just about sharing my story but rather helping others share their powerful story, whether it is one-on-one, to small groups, to thousands or to millions of people. I felt like I had received a promotion and couldn't be happier. One of my greatest joys is to help you grasp the power of your story so, you, too, can transform lives for His Kingdom.

After doing some research I discovered the top three questions people are asking when it comes to sharing their story are based on, "How can I be sure I even have a story, If I could come up with something, I don't know if anyone would want to hear it or I believe I have a story but have no idea how to get started."

Perhaps, these are your questions as well. Let me see if I can briefly address them. In the last 40 years I have helped thousands of people with their stories and the one thing that has been confirmed over and over is that everyone has a story. It's not just any story but a story that can transform lives. Unfortunately, we live in a broken world today. Therefore, people connect through pain, through problems and through conflict.

Every great story has conflict. Now, let me bring that closer to home. What conflict have you had? If I sat down with you over a cup of coffee, I know that with just asking you a few questions, I could help you find not just any story but a story that could transform lives just by exploring some of the conflicts you have faced.

Although story is used in many different ways, the key purpose of the kind of story I am referring to is to come alongside, identify with or connect with your listener. Keep in mind, although, you may be a natural storyteller, there is a skill to learning to tell stories effectively. Like any skill, it takes practice, practice, and more practice to learn it well.

You may be wondering how do I get started? I would like to give you three resources that will help you get started.

1. *Your Story Matters, Own Your Story and Tell It With Clarity, Confidence & Impact* is an easy read that will introduce you to the foundation of story. It gives you the 5 C's; clarity, creation, confidence, connection and courage, everything you need to create your powerful story. You can find it on Amazon at https://www.amazon.com/dp/0981901425/ref=cm_sw_em_r_mt_dp_EFVVH4CWDY4PA2M114E7
2. Download FTG (Fetch the Goodness) Network on ROKU and click on Wealth Through Stories. Here you will find powerful training based around story as well as great interviews as people share their story from a vulnerable heart. It is time to return to God's goodness as we learn more about story. (Note flyer at the back of the book).
3. Another great opportunity which is even more personal is Linda's 2-day Story Retreat. Just go to https://

wealththroughstories.com/story-reteat to find out more info and sign up. (Note the $100 coupon code on the flyer at the back of the book.)

When it comes to story, the question isn't whether you have a powerful story, it's valuing the power in your story. I would be honored to help you uncover the power of your story so together we can impact thousands, perhaps millions of lives. Just go to www.wealththroughstories.com and sign up for a FREE 20-min Story Strategy session.

Remember, Your Story Matters!

Linda Olson is a TEDx speaker, Story Expert and multiple bestselling Author. Her greatest joy is helping others find the wealth in their story so they can impact the people they were called to reach.

Are you **CONTINUALLY** plagued with **GUILT**?

Does **SHAME** drive you into deep emotional **DARKNESS**?

Have you **LOST ALL HOPE** of living freely, unhindered, and with great peace and joy?

PICK UP YOUR COPY AT AMAZON.COM

C.J. Schat, Amazon Best-selling author, shares the treasures she uncovered, after many painful years, in her book,
The Tree of Faith:
God Wants to Answer Your Prayer

In this book you will discover the:
- age-old secret to obliterating fear, guilt, and shame.
- personal way God answers questions.
- transforming power that heals deep wounds.
- unique key to turning life around.
- growing faith that looks past the impossible.

IS IT POSSIBLE TO
RISE ABOVE
THE
LONELINESS AND **DEPRESSION**
THAT YOU MAY BE FACING?

IS IT POSSIBLE TO
**ELIMINATE
ANGER, FEAR,** AND **INSECURITY**
IN THE MIDST OF GREAT LOSS?

Leena Ying Tang, Author, Speaker and award winning Realtor shares the secrets she grasped in overcoming life's harsh challenges in her book,

SOAR LIKE AN EAGLE
LET GO OF FEAR AND WORRY TO EMBRACE HOPE AND STRENGTH

IN THIS BOOK, LEENA SHOWS YOU:
- How to let go of FEAR and stand in confidence, courage & love.
- How to let go of WORRY and enjoy a peace that passes all understanding.
- How to embrace HOPE and know that all things are possible when we believe.
- How to embrace STRENGTH and mount up with wings like eagles.

Now is the time to own your story and say, "Yes" to God who makes the seemingly impossible, possible.

PICK UP YOUR COPY AT
Amazon.com

One Story
One Transformation

IMPACTING MORE LIVES THAN SHE EVER IMAGINED!

Facing the Storm with Kokoro

Like you, Hatsuki – Suki for short, faced situations in life where she wasn't sure which way to go because she couldn't see clearly. The pounding rain, horrendous thunder, and cracking lightning nearly drowned out all hope for survival. Soon she discovered that she always had a choice, and the first choice was always the most important one – It was seeking wisdom through her Kokoro (Spiritual heart). After much searching, she discovered how to steer her ship in such a way during a storm as to lead her to peaceful waters, full of hope and fulfillment that only God could bring.

Fight with Smile

Suki's struggle with cancer brought her to a big decision – to live or die. She chose LIFE. Today she is determined to live each day with a smile.

Sukorina

Suki introduces her Children's series. This series, an expression of Suki's writing and art, shares important values to instill in your children and grandchildren.

Hatsuki Murata, *a celebrated author and artist, lives in the high desert of Southern California and enjoys her friends, her family, and her readers. She has risen above the storms in life and is determined to live life with a smile using the gifts she has been given.*

moving mom and dad

5 Common Mistakes Adult Children of Aging Parents Make And How to Avoid Them

Adult children with **aging parents** report to not knowing the desires of their elder parents. Their perceptions are not in line with their **actual wishes**.

In the guide, *moving mom and dad*, we help to ease your load by walking you through a system that gives you wisdom and tips in this sensitive area.

In Six Steps you will discover:
1: Five common mistakes to avoid
2: Having the "What if" talk
3: Determining Priorities
4: Moving On
5: Dealing with the "stuff"
6: Assembling important documents

Joanne Peters, a public speaker and life coach for senior living, empowers the older generation to embrace memories and find joy in living the greatest chapter of their lives in order to leave intentional legacies that are without regret.

Meet Joanne on ROKU, FTG Network (Fetch the Goodness), *Wealth Through Stories*.
Her story is featured in Season 1: Episodes 8, 9 & 12.

Go to CentralCoastSenior.com to request a FREE consultation and receive your FREE guide, *moving mom and dad*.

An Invitation To

WEALTH THROUGH STORIES *Live*

"The question isn't whether you have a story, it's finding the POWER in your story."

$100 coupon — **WTS** *Live* — **$100 coupon**

use coupon code
wtsmember
when you purchase your ticket
wealththroughstories.com/story-retreat

At WTS LIVE you will discover:
- Creation of simple stories that can transform lives
- Clarity to create a story without the challenge, fear, & frustration most people face
- Confidence that your story matters & how to impact the people you want to reach
- Connection with how your story can meet the needs of the people you want to reach
- Courage to transform a life through your story in as little as 2 minutes

Linda Olson
CEO of Wealth Through Stories
TEDx Speaker/
3x #1 Bestselling Author

WTS
WEALTH THROUGH STORIES
Helping You Impact Millions With Your Story

Go to www.WealthThroughStories.com and sign up for a Complimentary Story Strategy session to find out how you can

Reach Millions with Your Story.

Wealth Through Stories
"IMPACTING MILLIONS THROUGH STORY"
WealthThroughStories.com

LINDA OLSON, #1 INTERNATIONAL BESTSELLING AUTHOR INVITES YOU TO JOIN HER ON A STORY JOURNEY

Does your story really MATTER?
Do you want to eliminate FEAR and INSECURITY?
Do you want to PIERCE the HEARTS of your target audience?

LEARN TO VALUE THE POWER IN YOUR STORY!

IN ONLY 15 MINUTES, ON HER TV SERIES ON ROKU, YOU WILL EXPERIENCE POWERFUL TRAININGS AS YOU GRASP THE VALUE OF STORY:

- What enables your heart to tell a better story?
- The secret to finding more stories than you can count
- Finding a story that matters
- The secret ingredient to story
- How can I live a great story?

LINDA OLSON is a TEDx speaker, Story Expert and Founder of Wealth Through Stories. Together with her husband, Rick, they enjoy two married daughters and five adorable grandchildren who are the best part of her story.

Join Linda and her guests on ROKU, FTG Network, (Fetch the Goodness), Wealth Through Stories. You will hear interviews with her special guests; ordinary people telling their extraordinary stories on ROKU.com.

Made in the USA
Monee, IL
24 December 2021